Additional Titles for N
American Acader

Baby and Toddler Basics: Expert Answers to Parents' Top 150 Questions

Baby Care Anywhere: A Quick Guide to Parenting On the Go

Caring for Your Baby and Young Child: Birth to Age 5*

Dad to Dad: Parenting Like a Pro

Food Fights: Winning the Nutritional Challenges of Parenthood
Armed With Insight, Humor, and a Bottle of Ketchup

Guide to Toilet Training

Heading Home With Your Newborn: From Birth to Reality

Mama Doc Medicine: Finding Calm and Confidence in Parenting,
Child Health, and Work-Life Balance

My Child Is Sick! Expert Advice for Managing Common Illnesses and Injuries

New Mother's Guide to Breastfeeding

The Picky Eater Project: 6 Weeks to Happier, Healthier Family Mealtimes

Raising an Organized Child: 5 Steps to Boost Independence,
Ease Frustration, and Promote Confidence

Raising Twins: Parenting Multiples From Pregnancy Through the School Years

Retro Baby: Cut Back on All the Gear and Boost Your Baby's Development
With More Than 100 Time-tested Activities

Retro Toddler: More Than 100 Old-School Activities to Boost Development

Sleep: What Every Parent Needs to Know

Understanding the NICU: What Parents of Preemies and Other
Hospitalized Newborns Need to Know

Your Baby's First Year*

healthychildren.org
Powered by pediatricians. Trusted by parents.

For additional parenting resources, visit the HealthyChildren
bookstore at https://shop.aap.org/for-parents.

*This book is also available in Spanish.

The New Baby Blueprint

Caring for You and Your Little One

WHITNEY CASARES, MD, MPH, FAAP

American Academy of Pediatrics
DEDICATED TO THE HEALTH OF ALL CHILDREN®

American Academy of Pediatrics Publishing Staff

Mary Lou White, *Chief Product and Services Officer/SVP, Membership, Marketing, and Publishing*
Mark Grimes, *Vice President, Publishing*
Holly Kaminski, *Editor, Consumer Publishing*
Shannan Martin, *Production Manager, Consumer Publications*
Amanda Helmholz, *Medical Copy Editor*
Peg Mulcahy, *Manager, Art Direction and Production*
Sara Hoerdeman, *Marketing Manager, Consumer Products*

Published by the American Academy of Pediatrics
345 Park Blvd
Itasca, IL 60143
Telephone: 630/626-6000
Facsimile: 847/434-8000
www.aap.org

The American Academy of Pediatrics is an organization of 67,000 primary care pediatricians, pediatric medical subspecialists, and pediatric surgical specialists dedicated to the health, safety, and well-being of infants, children, adolescents, and young adults.

The information contained in this publication should not be used as a substitute for the medical care and advice of your pediatrician. There may be variations in treatment that your pediatrician may recommend based on individual facts and circumstances.

Statements and opinions expressed are those of the authors and not necessarily those of the American Academy of Pediatrics.

Any websites, brand names, products, or manufacturers are mentioned for informational purposes only and do not imply an endorsement by the American Academy of Pediatrics (AAP). The AAP is not responsible for the content of external resources. Information was current at the time of publication.

The publishers have made every effort to trace the copyright holders for borrowed materials. If they have inadvertently overlooked any, they will be pleased to make the necessary arrangements at the first opportunity.

This publication has been developed by the American Academy of Pediatrics. The contributors are expert authorities in the field of pediatrics. No commercial involvement of any kind has been solicited or accepted in development of the content of this publication. Disclosures: The author reports no disclosures.

Every effort is made to keep *The New Baby Blueprint: Caring for You and Your Little One* consistent with the most recent advice and information available from the American Academy of Pediatrics.

Special discounts are available for bulk purchases of this publication. Email Special Sales at aapsales@aap.org for more information.

Printed in the United States of America

9-443   1 2 3 4 5 6 7 8 9 10

CB0116
ISBN: 978-1-61002-375-7
eBook: 978-1-61002-376-4
EPUB: 978-1-61002-377-1
Kindle: 978-1-61002-378-8
PDF: 978-1-61002-379-5

Cover design by Kelsey Cronkhite
Publication design by Peg Mulcahy
Illustration on page 99 by Tony LeTourneau. Reproduced with permission.

Library of Congress Control Number: 2019948087

What People Are Saying

Dr Casares has written a parenting manual that helps new and experienced caregivers of infants not just survive but thrive. Writing in an often humorous conversational style, Dr Casares comes across not only as a knowledgeable expert on newborn parenting but also as a life coach whose advice is sound, reassuring, evidence based, and inspirational!

> —Lewis First, MD, MS, FAAP, professor and chair, Department of Pediatrics, University of Vermont Larner College of Medicine; chief of pediatrics, University of Vermont Children's Hospital; and editor in chief, *Pediatrics*

In this internet age of numerous "experts" giving advice on parenting, Dr Casares, a skilled pediatrician and mother, distills down volumes of information into a single, easy-to-read guide. Her book is honest and practical—a fresh focus on the mother's needs as well as those of the infant. Her candidness about her own struggles with bringing her babies home, combined with her work with countless new mothers in her practice, informs this modern blueprint for the well-being of the professional mother and her family.

> —Nicole Cirino, MD, reproductive psychiatrist; director, Women's Mental Health Program, Oregon Health & Science University (OHSU) Center for Women's Health; and professor of obstetrics and gynecology and of psychiatry, OHSU

A wonderful, practical resource! With both the good sense of a mom who's "been there, done that" and the seasoned experience of a pediatrician who's helped hundreds of moms navigate the same journey, Dr Casares offers wise guidance and practical tips to parents of newborns. Easy to read, it strikes the right balance between an overall approach to parenting and practical advice on the nitty-gritty details. It's like having coffee with a best friend who, by the way, just happens to be an expert on all things related to new babies and new moms. I can't imagine a better baby shower gift.

> —Janelle Aby, MD, FAAP, author of *The Newborn Book: Significance of Physical Findings in the Neonate* and clinical professor of pediatrics at Stanford University School of Medicine

Pediatricians often get emails, texts, and calls from friends seeking parenting advice from someone with a pediatric medical background. Dr Casares wrote a book that meets this need! She blends practical parenting tips and medical knowledge in this fresh and fun perspective on parenting. It's a great read for any parent who is interested in the pediatrician-mom perspective!

> —Lauren Rose, MD, FAAP, newborn and pediatric hospitalist

Dr Casares shares her expertise on newborns from her professional roles as pediatrician and mom in a funny, practical, and down-to-earth manner. Her book provides the most practical advice for new moms that I have read...from preparing for the birth of the child to managing expectations of new moms and sharing her own personal experiences to giving parents-to-be all they need to know but were never told about having a baby. New moms everywhere will find this guide to being a parent invaluable and refer to it again and again.

> —Deborah Rumsey, executive director, Children's Health Alliance

Dedication

To my exhausting, amazing children, who have educated me in the ways of motherhood far more than any official training ever could. I wouldn't want my life any other way.

To my husband, who balances my enthusiasm and persistence with a steady dose of humor and reality.

And to my parents, who have always dreamed alongside me and for me, teaching me to value hard work and vision equally.

Contents

Preface

*The moment a child is born, the mother is also born.
She never existed before. The woman existed,
but the mother, never. A mother is something
absolutely new.*

—*Rajneesh*

Yesterday, I heard my almost-18-month-old toddler wake up, and I hurried upstairs to get her. She looked up, smiled a huge and toothy grin, and babbled some funny phrase about bananas and her bunny as she realized it was time to start the day. As I held her for the first time that morning, rubbing her back and gazing at her little fingers resting on her cheek, I thought, "How did I get so lucky?"

When my first child was born 4½ years ago, that would not have been my sentiment as a new parent. As a pediatrician, I knew what to expect medically with a new baby, but I still felt blindsided, at first, by the fatigue, stress, and emotions that come with being a new mom. My husband and I lovingly referred to our new daughter as a "hater": she "hated" the swing, the pacifier, the carrier, the baby wrap, the bassinet, the car safety seat, the bouncy chair, and the activity mat. I know this because we tried them all several times. We eventually nicknamed her Limoncello, in reference to the lemony Italian liquor, for her ability to be super sweet when peaceful yet strong and sour at many other times.

I started to wonder after a few weeks what was making her that way. Was I too anxious? Did I not have her on an adequate sleep schedule? Was there something I was eating, wearing, doing, or not doing? Would it ever end, and would I ever get sleep again?

My greatest joy in my pediatrics practice is working with new and expectant moms, helping them build confidence with their little ones and finding the resources they need. I see many consistent themes as women transition into motherhood, the most common of which is shock at the paradigm shift when they find themselves suddenly responsible not only for the well-being but also for the survival of another human being. And in spite of all the information out there, they still feel unprepared going into the whole baby thing.

Sure, moms-to-be learn a lot of tips and tricks about baby gear and birth plans, but because sometimes it's hard to think past what's right in front of them, they never get past the labor-and-delivery planning mind-set. After their baby arrives, they feel blindsided, alone, and sometimes frustrated with those who told them that "being a mom is hard" but never specifically said what was so hard and what could be done to make it easier.

Back in the throes of colic and tears (or even before they came), I wished that someone had sat me down and gone through what to expect in the first weeks and months in a very real, unfiltered way. So I started thinking about how to help other moms like me enter motherhood with the practical, realistic information they needed—the information I needed—about how to prepare themselves, their partners if they have one, and their families for the major change they were about to face.

The New Baby Blueprint: Caring for You and Your Little One is my best attempt at doing just that for you.

In this book, you will find the answers to the deeper questions you have about becoming a mom—the scary questions that all of us have. You know, the ones about how you are actually going to *do this*. And I think you'll find a lot of reality and reassurance.

The first 2 weeks, 2 months, and even 6 to 7 months will be tough with a little one. There is so much transition. The learning curve is incredibly steep. It can be intimidating, but in the end, there is joy—completely magical, over-the-top, amazing joy.

Importantly, although I focus on moms in this book and parent with my husband, the lifestyles and arrangements of families is diverse. Some information may apply to all parents—adoptive, dads, grandparents, parents of multiples, partners, same-sex, single, and others—or be adaptable. To learn more, talk with your pediatrician. In addition, information applies equally to babies and children of both sexes and all genders; however, to ease reading, I've chosen to alternate between masculine pronouns and feminine pronouns.

Acknowledgments

The New Baby Blueprint: Caring for You and Your Little One would not have been possible without the support and input of so many people. Special thanks to Mari Kay Evans-Smith, MD, and Bruce Birk, MD, my pediatrician colleagues who provided early content help and encouragement; to Ellen Portrait, RN, and Jennifer Siebold, NP, who provided initial feedback on lactation topics; to Reagan Cannon and Christie Artis, who helped with early website conceptualization; to Lauren Edmonds at Evernew Photography, who brought the Modern Mommy Doc and *The New Baby Blueprint* concept to life; to Aric Armon, who provided inspiration for the Modern Mommy Doc website and logo design; to Caroline Ghiossi, who gave me the current pregnant mom perspective; to Kelsey Cronkhite at Pinegate Road, my website designer who conceptualized the book cover design; to the talented Barbara Teszler at Teszler PR, Inc.; to the American Academy of Pediatrics (AAP) Publishing and Marketing teams, including Barrett Winston and my editor, Holly Kaminski; to Laura A. Jana, MD, Jennifer Shu, MD, and Joan Younger Meek, MD, my AAP peer reviewers; and to my husband, who has always been my best editor in chief.

CHAPTER 1

Preparing Your Mind

O n a typical morning, all I want is a cup of coffee: hot, dark coffee to start the day. But it often goes awry, as it did one particular morning during my second maternity leave. The baby was crying, the toddler was protesting, and despite doing my best, I still couldn't seem to stop the chaos. Nothing was going as planned.

It started with breakfast. I must have turned the stove up too high because the scrambled eggs cooked way too fast and looked a little charred. "Yuck. Those eggs are *not* fresh," said my older girl looking at her plate. "I would like peanut butter and jelly, not *that*!" Tears flowed as she flung herself to the ground out of protest, her plate nearly crashing to the floor with her.

Then, I went to change the little one's diaper, and poop came spewing out at me, faster than I could react. It shot into my hair; it peppered the sheets of my bed; it even ended up on the clean diapers I had placed next to her. It was everywhere. Like a bottle of mustard had exploded. It was disgusting.

But this is the job of any parent. Not always, but a lot of the time. There is a loss of control, a coming to terms with the reality that your rhythm or plans could be thrown off at any moment by the needs or whims of your child. That change can be hard to come to grips with before it becomes your reality.

If you are like me, you've had a job, you've traveled, and you have somewhat (or a lot) of a social life. When your kids come, that tends to change a little bit, but it's not forever. You don't have to lose yourself when you become a parent. You do, however, have to adjust your expectations. You will have fun again, you will have date nights, and you will, at some point (kind of), get back to who you were before you became, for example, Mommy or Daddy.

Right now, it's time to dig in your heels and expect many tough days and nights. You're in store for moments of complete bliss, to be sure, but being a parent can seem, well, annoying at times. You don't have your freedom, you lose control of your schedule, and you get lost in a sea of feeding and pooping and sleeping—then you do it all again the very next day. Is it hard? You betcha. Is it worth it? *Absolutely.*

Better to be mentally prepared for a period of awkward transition than to expect smooth sailing from the get-go. Becoming a parent, just like starting any new and challenging job, usually involves a steep learning curve. Here are my top tips for preparing your mind before your baby's arrival.

Accept chaos

Embrace that your home will not be a serene haven of adult life for several years. If you have toys and play mats and kids' stuff all around, do not stress out that your house will never be as neat and tidy as it once was. It won't be. That's life. Congratulations, you have a child now! Where there was serenity, there will now be a little being, full of joy and life (and noise and mess).

Instead of aiming for peace and quiet, figure out how to get ahold of yourself when you're stressed-out by your little one's cry or your chaotic environment. Amazingly, your neurons are completely connected to your newborn's at birth, so it pays in a multitude of ways to find calm. No pressure, right? But your level of stress or nonstress influences your baby's disposition.

What can you do about it when the scrambled eggs are burning and the diapers are overflowing?

Imagine yourself sitting on top of a huge glass bubble. Inside it, you and your child are having your moment. You can see what's going on, but you're not a part of it; instead, you're an observer. You notice what's going on, but it's going on in front of you, not to you, as if you're watching yourself in a movie. Suddenly, as you breathe and observe, you're not so caught up in how horrible everything seems right then. You have emotional distance and gain some objectivity.

Yogis and psychologists call this *meditating;* I call it "out of the bubble." It's a concrete example for removing yourself emotionally from the situation—even just for a moment—so that you can gain a little perspective.

Of course, breathing in and out and using imagery will not solve every problem you will ever have as a parent, and you may not even be able to use this strategy every time you have a chaotic day. When you can use it, though, you'll feel yourself relax and develop mindfulness. You'll build resilience in yourself and your kids as they watch you learn how to cope in stressful situations.

Using breathing and mindfulness is an amazing trick for reducing stress in new parents specifically, because those early dog days of parenting sometimes seem never-ending.

You'll hear the clichés from those who have already lived it: "It'll be over before you know it. That time is so precious;

don't wish it away." Of course, they'll be right. But until you make it over that steep, dry mountain of early parenting, into to the lush, green (in some ways easier) valley that's waiting for you, it won't feel brief, or precious, or wistful. It will feel, literally, like eggs and spit-up all over your hair. Learn to laugh and breathe. It's all you can do.

Give yourself a break

When Jenny came into the office with her 2 boys to see me for their health supervision visits, she looked exhausted. She'd been up all night worried about a diaper rash her youngest developed a few days prior. The moment she noticed the rash, Jenny used a product someone gave her as a sample on her most recent trip to the makeup counter at a major department store.

She watched the rash become worse and worse, so she kept on applying the cream. Each time she did, the rash seemed to spread farther and farther. Her baby was fussy all day long and he couldn't sleep well at night. The possibility an ingredient in the cream was the reason his skin seemed to be getting more and more angry didn't even cross her mind. At 1:00 am the night before her doctor appointment with me, the realization that she'd made a mistake woke her from a deep sleep.

Jenny jolted out of bed, ran to her son's crib, and immediately placed him into a warm bath. She stayed up an additional 2 hours researching every ingredient in the lotion sample and thinking about how she wished she had immediately asked for advice on how to treat the skin condition instead of quickly applying the first thing she could find. Jenny felt even more guilt that she didn't immediately connect the worsening rash with the adult cream.

Eight hours later, we were sitting in my office; the rash was already better, but Jenny's emotions were still fragile.

"Why didn't I put two and two together faster?" she asked me. Her son was fine, but she was shaken. We used a good portion of that visit talking about giving ourselves grace as we parent.

All parents have moments when they worry more than they want to or don't parent like a pro (or even like their more experienced parent friends do). The most confident parents learn quickly to give themselves a break if they don't do things "just right."

There will be times you will plan an outing only to realize you should have stayed in. One day, you will scrounge around in your diaper bag while out to lunch with a wailing, pee-soaked baby and realize you have no more diapers. A day will come when you realize you totally missed the boat on why your baby was so fussy. Accept this and move on. We all do that stuff. Seasoned parents *continue* to do that stuff.

Even doctors who have children aren't perfect. One of my pediatrician partners didn't realize his daughter's wrist was broken for a week, until she finally told him, "I need an X-ray." I missed my daughter's case of pinworms (yes, you read that right) for a whole month. If you feel confused or regretful early on, you're in good company. Just remember, when you feel that you have messed up, you will also have learned something, and you'll be better at it tomorrow.

One day, you'll think you have it all figured out

There will be a day when you think you have it all figured out. Then everything will change again, and you'll need to go back to the drawing board.

As your baby grows, the tricks that worked to help her sleep, to entertain her, and to help her grow will evolve as she does. One day, she'll love the swaddle blanket; one day later, it will be the sleep sack. The change in preference will not be the big deal—it will be the 2 weeks it takes to figure out the issue keeping her (and you) awake all night. The good news is that as you get to know your little nugget, those transitions will become easier and easier.

The most successful new parents I meet try not to (1) expect things to always stay the same, (2) get irritated by every developmental stage a child goes through, or (3) expect the transition through those stages to progress in a straight line, instead of a messy zigzag.

Getting irritated at each developmental stage is a trap commonly seen with first-time moms and dads and other parents, but "second timers" fall into it from time to time too, especially when they have more than one kid to juggle. I see it a lot in my practice. Although many new parents understand quickly that feeding troubles and sleepless nights are just part of the game, some bang their heads against the wall with what seems like shock and terror as each new developmental stage (and headache) arises.

They can't seem to accept that certain childhood behaviors are just a typical part of growing up. And although I'm impressed by their tenacious desire and willingness to problem-solve, sometimes I think they've been misled along the way by past advice or by society.

I bestow upon you, a parenting pearl: yes, parents can prevent and address a lot of health issues that come up for newborns, infants, and young kids, but some issues (such as cluster feeding, sleep regressions, and colic) are more about muddling through with the right perspective than they are about finding quick-fix solutions. Some things just take time to get better. (Major caveat here: If you have a serious health concern about your child or are worried about her safety or about potential illness, contact your child's doctor right away. Don't ever hesitate to contact your baby's pediatrician regarding your concerns for your baby.)

Banish Mommy guilt

Katie knows all about Mommy guilt. She's a lawyer at a successful firm in town and she works more than 50 hours per week. She's used to working extra in the evenings and on the weekends to finish all she has to do if she can't fit it in during business hours. Sometimes she has early meetings or late-night events with community partners that she can't miss.

Before she became a mom, Katie never thought much about how much she worked. In fact, she loved working, especially when she had a particularly difficult case. The problem-solving opportunities and interpersonal challenges she faced every day energized her. She was known as a super-star within her organization and within her particular area of expertise.

When her first child was born, though, things suddenly changed for Katie. She still loved her job as much as she always had, but now she had a precious baby who also needed her love, attention, and time. When she returned to the workforce at the end of her maternity leave, and left her newborn with a caregiver most of the day, she felt extremely guilty.

"I've never felt so conflicted about anything in my life," she told me one day during a visit with her kids. "I'm used to handling tough situations with confidence, but the level of guilt I experienced really surprised me."

Over time, Katie found ways to address those Mommy guilt feelings head-on and to make decisions so that each of her priorities—her kids and her job—received the time and energy they deserved.

"Dealing with Mommy guilt was one of the most critical skills I learned as a new mom," she told me a few years later as she explained how she'd grown in this area over time.

Mommy guilt is one of the worst-feeling parenting issues. There you are, perfect little baby in hand, and *wham!*—in will come Mommy guilt, making you feel like a failure when you're not producing enough milk, taunting you when you leave your baby for the first time, gnawing at you, or making you feel as if you must not be doing enough to stimulate, soothe, protect, and what have you your little one.

It can be worse when they start to get a little older. When my youngest daughter turned 1 year old, she perfected the "Mommy, don't go" cry, which usually consisted of "Mom, Mom, Mom, Mom, Mom, Mom" over and over again while she clung to my pant leg. It regularly happened when I was heading out to my job in the morning or when I was all geared up to work out. It hardly ever happened to my husband (I'm sure it did, but I just didn't notice it, because I have room in my brain for only my guilt, not his as well). It was even enough to make me cry in my car occasionally.

What are our choices as modern mothers when Mommy guilt comes barging in?

The Martyr Route

We could never take time for ourselves. Never take the time to hang out with friends. Never take an adult vacation. Never feel as if we're inconveniencing our partners or other caregivers.

It's an option I see a lot of parents take. I could too. But I know where that path leads us, and it's dark and lonely and kind of muddy.

Mommy guilt itself doesn't serve us well. We're less healthy physically and mentally. We're faster to get irritated and lose our cool with the kids. Let's face it—it's a pretty sad example of the balance we hope our children will have in their own lives.

The Balanced Route

When we prioritize ourselves as much as we do with other people and obligations in our lives, we can figure out what the real issue is and what scares us so much.

As you think about your new baby coming into the world, consider this one of the major parenting philosophy choices you make. Just like you'll set an example for your children to be kind and to be hardworking, you'll also set an example when it comes to balance and perspective.

Now, somewhere along the way, someone (ie, usually a partner or an older family member) is going to make you question your decision to make self-care a priority.

We live in a society in which perfect motherhood is mysti-fied and celebrated and expected to happen on its own. Our social media posts are just a little too glossy and polished. Some celebrities make motherhood seem like a goddess dream. Magazines sell us on the fake assumption that if we get all the right gear and plan it all out, we'll get an A+ in parenting class. Set that in contrast with the messy reality of our day-to-day lives—we're bound to be uneasy and a bit ashamed.

Overwhelmed by the Motherhood Goddess Myth herself, New York City mom Margaret Nichols said it well when she spoke about the pressure to do things just right in a *Time* magazine cover story: "What I've learned is there are some things you can control, but there is a lot you can't. We just have to give ourselves a break and do the best we can."

Self-care does not mean going out every single night 'til dawn; it refers to taking consistent time for ourselves to regroup and reboot. Where is the evidence that working or taking some time for self-care actually damages our kids? Wait for it...*it's not there.*

There are 3 concepts to keep in mind.

PROVIDE CONSISTENCY

Your baby will learn early on that she has people in her life who love her. She doesn't need those people to be around her constantly. She just needs those people to make special time to connect with her consistently. As your child grows, this will mean providing planned moments to connect with your child that she can count on throughout the week. For now, though, it simply means spending a few mindful moments with her throughout the day. It means paying special attention to her by singing to her or talking to her.

BE FOCUSED

Sound a little too easy? Technology unfortunately sometimes makes this a difficult task. Paying focused attention to your baby means you'll need to take care of what you need to do and then put away, for example, the smartphone so that the time you spend with your baby is purposeful instead of distracted. Your baby needs undivided attention at regular intervals throughout the day, without a screen in between you and him. Read your email when your baby is asleep instead of when he's wide awake in your arms. When you're feeding your baby, use the opportunity to tell him how much you love him (or just about what you're noticing within the room). In doing so, you'll start a special relationship with your child.

SHARE THE LOAD

Allow other caregivers in your baby's life to be equal players who provide the same level of consistency you do. I promise, they will rise to the occasion and have a stronger relationship with your baby as a result.

On some weekends, my husband makes waffles and takes the kids to the park while I do something solo. The next morning, we switch, and I do something special with them. Each parent gets time to reboot, and we're less resentful of the other's free time; plus, we get some individual moments with our kids to make memories.

Mommy (and Daddy) guilt will be hard to avoid, but the reality is that it just doesn't do any of us good. Take care of yourself physically and mentally so that you can take care of the other people in your life with an equal measure of love and commitment.

CHAPTER 2

"Gearing" Up

My husband won't let me live one particular memory down. We were out on our first lunch date "post-baby" with the little one in tow. We had just come from the doctor's office, 2 days into doing this on our own without the doting of hospital nurses, and although we were a little intimidated, we followed the advice of our pediatrician and braved a not-so-crowded restaurant in the middle of the day for burgers and fries.

We were there for less than an hour, and our daughter slept the entire time, but onlookers must have thought we were planning to stay the weekend: we brought along a mini breastfeeding pillow, 6 diapers, 2 packs of wipes, a breastfeeding cover, hand sanitizer, an extra swaddle blanket (or 3), a small white-noise machine, the stroller, and, of course, the car safety seat. I have a picture of myself from that day, sheepishly smiling into the camera.

Looking back, it was hilarious. All my stuff barely fit onto the bench beside my baby. We didn't use any of the items we carted in from the back of the car other than the car safety seat, where our newborn lay quietly snoozing, oblivious to our being overly prepared.

Baby Gear You Should Invest in Now

A few weeks prior, I had been in nesting mode, reading review after review about the perfect this and the perfect that and what other baby items I needed to get. When my mom came to our house and saw that we registered for a wipe warmer, she burst out laughing.

"You're kidding me, right? No baby needs that."

But I was convinced, just like most parents-to-be who get sucked into the billion-dollar baby business brouhaha, that I needed it all. However, when I donated all the unused baby items a few years later, preparing for my second child to arrive, I finally believed her advice: you are going to get and buy a ton of stuff when your new baby is born. You won't need most of it. If you end up needing it, it's usually only a click away.

Here's my list of the top 10 things I recommend investing in before your bundle of joy arrives.

One Small Box of Newborn Diapers

You don't know how big your baby will be, and you'll have buyer's remorse if you have a storage shed full of newborn diapers when your new baby is now a size 1 within a week of birth. You can *always* get more quickly.

Tons of Wipes

Babies poop. A lot. While purchasing too many itty-bitty diapers can be a waste, you'll never regret buying extra wipes. Eventually, you *will* use them. Start off with at least 5 boxes and plan to put them onto your shopping list again soon after your baby's birth. Look for wipes without added fragrances and pick thicker over thinner wipes when possible. Consider buying these items online where you can purchase them in bulk and possibly save a little money.

Vitamin D Drops

Breastfed babies need 400 IU (international units) of vitamin D per day until they reach 1 year of age. If your baby is drinking formula, check with your pediatrician about how much vitamin D to give.

Swaddle Blankets

I love the look of silky swaddle blankets, and these can serve a number of purposes such as a car safety seat cover or diaper change pad in a pinch, burp cloth, or breastfeeding cover. For swaddling a baby, blankets that are a little less slippery tend to be a better choice. Swaddle blankets tend to become dirty quickly because they're used for so many miscellaneous purposes. You'll want to have at least 5 when your baby is born so that you always have a clean one on hand when the rest are in the wash.

Zip-Up Sleepers and Onesies

Stick with zip-up sleepers at night. No snaps, no buttons. When your baby is a newborn, you want easy access to all those poopy diapers, especially at 2:00 am. I will never forget my husband fumbling with my daughter's tiny snaps in the middle of the night, mumbling under his breath about the makers of such "ridiculous getups." He was right. Lose the fancy clothes until about 3 months.

Onesies are also game changers, as newborns tend to go through multiple outfits a day, especially if they pee and poo and spit up all over them. Instead of having to do laundry all the time, have many onesies on hand so that you can easily swap out his dirty one for a clean one.

A Bassinet

Many parents use a bassinet next to their bed instead of a crib for the first few weeks after birth for easy feeding during the night. If you choose this option, make sure the bassinet has a Children's Product Certificate from the US Consumer Product Safety Commission.

The American Academy of Pediatrics recommends all parents and caregivers share a room with their baby for the first 6 months after birth and, ideally, for up to 1 year. That means you may not use your fancy crib for quite some time after your baby is born. You'll want convenience as a new mom, not aesthetics. Still, it's more convenient to arrange your newborn's nursery and assemble his crib before he arrives.

A Car Safety Seat

There are *tons* of options out there. After a few months, you'll probably end up taking your baby out of the car safety seat to carry him around, so, my best advice is, don't overthink it. Lots of companies work hard to sell you on features such as longevity or lightness, but babies outgrow car safety seats very quickly. They usually don't meet the upper weight limit before you are using a bigger seat they'll ride in through toddlerhood. Plus, even the lightest car safety seat will feel as if it weighs a ton once you have a baby in it. Remember that the safest place to position the car safety seat for a baby is in the middle of the back seat, with the baby facing the rear of the car. Also, make sure the car safety seat is buckled into the car securely every time you use it.

A Stroller

Two features matter most when it comes to strollers. Make sure it works with your car safety seat and is easy to fold and store in your car. My favorite strollers can be used for a long time, are easy to maneuver, and are easy to collapse and expand. Strollers are notoriously awkward to lift into and out of vehicles, so consider this as you decide between heavier models and lighter models. Just remember that you never want to run with a baby in a stroller until he is 6 months old, *even if* the stroller is advertised as a jogging stroller, to avoid serious neck and head injuries.

A Changing Table

You can change a baby's diaper pretty much anywhere—and you will in a pinch as a new mom—but when you are home, you'll want a designated place for this. The most efficient changing tables include spaces to store diapers, wipes, and diaper creams. If it makes financial sense for your family and you have a multilevel home, invest in a changing table for each floor of your house. This will allow you to avoid unnecessary trips up and down the stairs.

Breast Pump and Accessories

Oh man, we have a lot to talk about here (and in the next section!). When it comes to babies, there is a ton of baby gear you just *do not need.* But when it comes to breastfeeding, more is more. Pumps and accessories can be extremely helpful in the first year after your baby's birth, especially if you're a working mom planning on feeding your little one pumped breast milk once you head back to your job.

Insurance companies will often pay for a pump, but look closely at the options they give you. You may need to upgrade to one that fits your needs so that you have one that will actually work for you. It's an investment, but if I were choosing between a pricey crib and a pricey breast pump, I would *always* choose the breast pump. It's not quite as fun to look at, but it will make your life significantly easier.

Breastfeeding Gear

Setting Up Your Breastfeeding Gear

Understandably, one of the biggest mistakes I see moms-to-be make is not to have their breastfeeding gear (breast pump and its coordinating parts) all set up before they have their baby. Yes, you can do it afterward, but if feeding is not going well and you need to use it, the last thing you want to do is spend time messing around with sanitizing pump equipment.

It is important for the breast pump to be a double-electric pump, which means you can pump both breasts at the same time, and to have an electric motor, preferably with an adjustment for different suction levels.

It also needs to work with a breast pump system, which means it's compatible with bottles for feeding, bottles for storing milk, cleaning supplies, cooler bags, freezer bags, and other gear. You want all this to work seamlessly together so that you don't use your priceless time jury-rigging a ton of junk together.

One hidden consideration? Your pump needs to have easy-to-find replacement parts. Most of the major brands out there should qualify. If the pump parts are not readily available online or at the store, you'll become frantic when you really need an accessory and you can't find one.

Most important—and this is not emphasized enough—you need something that is going to be *portable*. When I had my first daughter, I had this huge pump that needed to be plugged into a wall at all times to work. I quickly switched over to one that had extreme portability. (For some moms with production issues, the pump efficiency is the most important factor, making other considerations seem frivolous. Follow your pediatrician's and a lactation specialist advice.) Whichever setup you choose, most important is that you set the gear up and have it all sterilized *before* you have your baby. This is an awesome task to assign to a partner, but, you'll be using it, so make sure you have a working knowledge of the pump yourself.

Setting Up Your Breastfeeding Space

When buying your baby gear, consider where you will feed your baby. On the couch? In a rocking chair? Make sure that wherever you choose allows you to have 90° angles at your hips and your knees when you are feeding and has a wide enough space so that you can accommodate you, your baby, and a breastfeeding pillow when you are starting out. A lot of the fancy nursery chairs are too narrow to do that. Bring the feeding pillow to the store when you are trying to find a breastfeeding chair. Don't forget about the furniture you already have in your house too—the couch can sometimes be your best option. Often a step stool at your feet can allow you to get into the right 90°-90° positioning as well.

Choosing a Feeding Pillow

In the first few weeks to months, your new baby will be small and you will not be used to breastfeeding. A breastfeeding pillow can be extremely helpful in positioning your baby. This is especially true for moms who have cesarean deliveries. For all moms, a breastfeeding pillow can assist you with maintaining a more upright position during feedings. Staying relaxed and reclined allows you to prevent neck and back strain, can help if you have overactive letdown issues, and generally will make life easier.

There are a number of different options, but check out product reviews and look for one that it is more supportive for your baby. The goal is to get your baby to nipple level.

Sometimes you have to add a blanket underneath the pillow to raise it up. This is also an item that you could easily borrow from a friend, especially if the cover is washable.

When to Use a Bottle

Most experts agree that at about 3 to 4 weeks of age, a baby using a bottle once a day or every other day will not compromise breastfeeding success. Until then, wait on using bottles unless instructed to use them by your pediatrician or lactation specialist.

If your baby has been evaluated and needs an extra supplement of pumped breast milk, your pediatrician or lactation specialist can suggest special techniques to help keep your baby from developing a preference for taking breast milk from a bottle instead of from a breast (such as finger feeding, a supplemental breastfeeding system, or a special bottle known as a Haberman Specialized Feeder, which can be used to reduce reliance on a bottle).

Choosing the Right Nipple Size

One tip I learned early on? Babies sometimes prefer the bottle because the breast milk flows out of it a lot faster than it does from the breast (depending on the breast). However, this can also lead to more spit-ups and tummy aches. You may need to experiment with which nipple size works best for your baby.

For my first little one, I found that if I used the "preemie" nipple, it made her much more comfortable. For my second, it didn't matter which nipple we used—she was happy just to have the breast milk however it came. Don't be afraid to go down a size on the nipple if you feel as if your baby is having trouble with fast flow.

Using a Hand Pump

A hand pump is a nonelectric device you can use to quickly pump without having to set up your whole pump system. It's awesome for a number of uses and very portable. It's especially helpful if you unexpectedly need to pump and don't have a charged electric pump or a power outlet readily available.

Hand pumps are lighter, quieter, and cheaper than electric breast pumps. They're most useful for occasional pumping sessions, whereas electric pumps are generally faster at expressing larger breast milk volumes.

OVERACTIVE LETDOWN

If your first letdown sends your milk spraying all over your little one's face and looks like a torrential downpour or your baby seems to have a hard time handling the flow, you may have overactive letdown. Check with a lactation specialist to see if this is true for you.

One trick I've learned is to attach the sterilized hand pump (and use it to get the first few letdowns' worth of milk). This way, you're not so completely full of milk when your baby starts to eat and it is more comfortable for both of you.

ENGORGEMENT

In the first few days, it can be tough for your new baby to latch because your breast tissue is so tense. Sometimes a hand pump will help. Occasionally, you need your full-on double-electric breast pump for this, but it can often be easier, for both of you, to whip out the hand pump and pump off a few ounces.

What to Do About All Those Baby Gifts

We've talked about the top 10 things you really need for your newborn. But what about all those presents you'll receive? Just between us, you probably don't need or want all of them. The tricky part is, you often won't know if you need them until you reach that stage. If something is for sure not your style, return it right away—you don't want extra baby things to organize. If you're not sure and it's something the store always has in stock, take it back and get a gift card. Babies cost a lot to take care of—having gift cards on hand to buy the things you really need (or want) can be a lifesaver.

Helen understands full well what it means to overstock one's house in the name of preparedness only to feel over-whelmed. She's a mom of 2 elementary school kids now but still recalls setting up a baby registry at 3 separate stores before her first child was born. She worried that if she didn't have all the baby gear she needed ahead of time, she wouldn't have enough energy to find the items later.

Helen had multiple baby showers—one with work friends, one with family, and one with her closest girlfriends. Almost everyone purchased items off Helen's wish list and there were a lot of items. What they didn't gift her, she pur-chased herself, anxious her new baby might need something in the middle of the night those first few weeks and she would be left feeling helpless. She removed the packaging and put it all away. So everything was organized and had its place.

"I probably only used half of what they purchased," she told me in the office, thinking back to those early days. "After about 2 months, I understood how few baby things were actually useful, but it was too late to take much back. I wished I had had less at the beginning so I had more money to buy what I really needed (or wanted on a whim) later on."

Simplifying Your Newborn Gear Experience

You know the feeling when you go on vacation and you over-pack? The way your bag gets heavier and heavier the longer you lug it through the airport, into the rental car, and through the resort lobby?

That's how it feels (times 10) when you fill your house with too much baby gear. Diapers, baby swing, and baby toys: they can all be purchased online and delivered to your home for a small fee. Have a friend set up an online meal calendar so that friends can bring warm meals to nourish your family. This is the time to take advantage of a few modern conveniences. Really, you have more important things to do than drive around town running errands, such as sleep and bonding with your baby.

The inevitable kid chaos just multiplies with the more stuff you purchase. Your outings feel more burdensome, your house feels more cluttered, and experiences that should be very straightforward (such as going out to lunch for burgers and fries) suddenly feel very complicated. Keep it simple, and you'll be happier.

CHAPTER 3

Finding a Pediatrician

O ne mom I eventually came to know was about 5 months into the whole parenthood thing when she began to crumble. Every day, she woke with the hope that her little bundle of joy would decide that night (even if just for one night) to "sleep like a baby." And every night, she ended up rocking him back and forth for hours or shushing him loudly to the rhythm of the white-noise machine. Five months.

She found me through my practice's website and a friend's referral right around that time. She said she hadn't really thought much about who her baby's doctor would be before he actually arrived, but when things got tough, she realized all her Google searches weren't leading to any real answers. When she came to see me for the first time, exhausted and ready to quit, I could tell that she was fresh out of hope. I've known that mom now for almost 6 years. She has a funny, handsome kindergartener who sleeps every night in his own bed **all night long**. We're a good team, she and I. And she'll tell anyone who will listen, "It really matters who helps you along in the beginning."

Many pediatricians will offer a complimentary prenatal visit during which they meet with you to talk about the specifics of their practice. Call potential providers to find out. Make sure to ask all the questions you have on your mind.

Where do you find an amazing pediatric provider? Querying friends is an excellent place to start. Your obstetrician and local hospital can also serve as referral sources. If you're feeling stuck, ask your health insurance company—it will have a list of in-network pediatricians taking new patients in your area. Once you've identified a few top contenders, go online to check out candidates' websites, then set up a prenatal interview to see which expert is the best fit.

Finding a pediatrician can seem like a daunting task, but 5 main features tend to set stellar pediatric specialists apart from their peers.

The Office Practice

Look at the specifics of the practice in which you're interested. Does it have weekend or holiday hours? Are nurses available to answer questions you may have (even if those questions come in the middle of the night)? What are the extra services it has—is there a lactation specialist, a dietitian, or another specialist? Behavioral health providers? How up-to-date is its technological setup? Can you make your own appointments? Can you email your provider?

Experience and Certifications

Research the experience and board-certification status of the pediatrician you are choosing. All doctors who are certified to practice medicine by the American Board of Pediatrics have to pass examinations regularly, to keep up-to-date on continuing medical education, and to graduate from an accredited 4-year medical school program and 3-year pediatric residency program.

Your Level of Need

Make sure that the person you choose can accommodate your level of attention and need. Some parents are pretty laid back. They obviously care about their babies and want the best for them, but they generally take the information medical professionals give them at face value and don't need extended conversations with their providers about each decision they make. Other parents need more of an explanation, time, and information to feel heard and confident. Knowing what basket you fall into, or if you are somewhere in the middle, is extremely important.

The "Let's Get Real" Factor

In my opinion, finding a pediatrician who can look you in the eye and tell you an honest opinion, giving you real, practical information you can use, is invaluable. All board-certified pediatricians are familiar with up-to-date medical care guidelines for children, but some of my best doctor mentors specifically stand out for their ability to connect sincerely with parents and patients.

Especially as a new parent, you're going to have a lot of questions, and you can't feel rushed or hesitant to ask your pediatrician. Some of them will have black-and-white answers. "Should I take my 3-day-old newborn camping?" Absolutely not. Most of them, though, will be in a gray area. You want someone who can present the pros and cons of your choices clearly and with confidence so that you can make the best decisions possible.

Whole-Health Focus

Make sure the practice and pediatrician you choose focuses not only on physical health but also on social, developmental, and mental health. Your pediatrician should track your baby's growth but should also track her developmental milestones, intervening with extra support services if she needs them along the way. The best pediatricians also pay close attention to social determinants of health (the conditions in which people are born, grow, work, and age) and help parents connect with resources to promote their patients' overall health. Savvy pediatricians care that your little one grows in height and weight but also that she reaches her full potential when it comes to developing lifelong skills such as building resilience and learning how to make healthy life choices. They know that fostering resilience is possible even starting in the newborn period.

In our clinic, we have on-site psychologists and a dietitian who team up with us to maximize health holistically. We partner with other pediatricians in the community to compare clinic strategies and maintain the highest level of quality possible. Every 3 months, we review current research and recommendations from experts in the pediatric field.

Our pediatricians also meet regularly to discuss behavioral health and resilience with our mental health professional so that we are current on best care practices for our patients. We work to be integrated, providing the best care possible in a way that fits the unique needs of our patients and their caregivers. Staff, parents, and providers all give input as we design workflows and projects.

Will choosing the right pediatrician solve all your parenting woes and make your parenting journey pain-free? Of course not. Is a perfect pediatrician or pediatrics practice out there? No way. (I'll fully admit to that as a member of this specialty area.) Can you move through your early parenting experience knowing you have the support and knowledge base of someone who knows a ton about your child's health and cares a ton about your parenting success? Absolutely.

Pediatrician Interview Checklist

Board-certified Pediatrician Status

Availability and Access
- ☐ Phones
- ☐ Email
- ☐ Office hours
- ☐ Advice nurses
- ☐ Website
- ☐ Urgent and same-day appointments

Clinic Reputation
- ☐ Longevity of practice
- ☐ Unique features: dietitians, psychologists, lactation specialists, and other specialists

Experience
- ☐ Years in practice
- ☐ Training background and special areas of expertise

Hospital Privileges and Affiliations
- ☐ Do providers come see babies in the hospital?
- ☐ Local emergency department recommendations.

Book and Website Recommendations

What to Expect at Clinic
- ☐ Appointments in first 3 days
- ☐ Appointments in first 2 weeks

CHAPTER 4

Taking Care of You and Your Partner

*J*ulia was a social butterfly before she had kids. Almost every night after work, she met up with friends or went for a long run along the river in her town with her partner. She enjoyed taking ceramics classes at the local community college with an equally artistic coworker and even organized a pottery painting party for her best friend's birthday.

She and her husband loved exploring together. They especially enjoyed finding camping spots in the summer with amazing views.

"The way we traveled would be almost impossible with young children," she said. "We'd leave early in the morning before sunrise, pitch our tent, hang up a hammock, and then just relax together with a few good books. Our adventures were the ultimate in freedom and spontaneity. We could do whatever we wanted."

*Julia told me all about her life without babies or toddlers
at a baby expo where I spoke with moms-to-be about what
to expect emotionally once they became parents.*

*"I was still me after I had a baby," Julia said. My interests
and personality didn't change, but my life sure did. We still
traveled, but there was less freedom. I still socialized, but
I had to purposefully make time for it. New moms need to
know that motherhood means a shift in your physical self,
your emotional self, and your partner relationships. At first,
that was a hard transition to make. I felt a little lost. I was
surprised by the emotions that hit me."*

Sometimes I fell into the trap of emotions as a new mom
like Julia did.

*Bitter, sad, disappointed. Pining away for something else.
For what? For some other version of this life. For more of the
parts of life I actually enjoy. For space to breathe. For space to
enjoy. For freedom. Before having kids, it was restlessness for the
next step of life that kept me pining. Now it's a longing for time
to be mine when I am off work, to not be jealous when Dad gets
time away. For all of it. I want time to be by myself, but once
I have it, I squander it. I'm so tired. I miss my freedom. I miss
myself. It's unsustainable.*

So many new parents I meet are in this same boat, usually after the shine wears off at about the 2-week or 1-month
mark postpartum. Adrenaline can take you only so far, and
when that dissipates, it can be rough.

So many new moms are feeling desperate, and trapped,
and broken, not only when it comes to the relationship
with their partner but also when it comes to their sense of
self. Having a baby is a huge transition and it can be difficult to prepare for no matter how much you research and
read. It will inevitably change your relationship with your
partner, and it will definitely challenge the self-directed,

freedom-loving paradigm you know now, especially if you are a working mom-to-be and are climbing the corporate ladder. It's stressful to be a new mom, to say the absolute least. If you are experiencing these feelings, talk with your doctor as soon as possible so that you can get the help you need.

Review these motivating thoughts before your baby comes to help ease the transition.

Designate a soother in chief

Your partner is your soother in chief. Count on your partner to be the expert on the soothing techniques I talk about in the upcoming chapters. If you are breastfeeding, you have a full-time job that requires rest, fluids, and patience to learn and perfect. You are the feeder in chief. You'll do your fair share of soothing as a function of that job. But your partner should take the lead on soothing so that you can accomplish your main mission: feeding your baby. If you are single parenting, gather trusted friends or family members to help calm and hold your baby early on. Make a list of members in your support circle and keep it easily accessible so that you can call on others when you are struggling.

Give bonding some time

Understand that if your partner takes longer than you do to bond with your baby, it will come in due time.

My husband was always loving and in love with our daughter. He played with her and cuddled her every day in her first weeks. But just recently, he said, "It was when she started laughing and reacting to me that I felt connected to her. That's when we bonded."

Looking back now, it's true. About a month in, he started asking me to send him pictures when he was at work and

I was home with her. He started feeling sad when she was already asleep for the night by the time he got home and he couldn't participate in her bedtime routine. He missed her, and he didn't just love her now; he liked her too! If you give your partner that chief soothing job, this will come faster.

You're not a magician

Accept that you are not a magician and cannot develop a mom's intuition overnight. You need your partner's help, and (sometimes, believe it or not) partners have valid ideas! My husband learned this relatively early, thank goodness, with some gentle coaching from experienced dads in our friend group and his own father. When my baby was crying at 6 weeks old and I had fed, rocked, shushed, and swayed her for hours with no end in sight, I needed another set of hands to give me a break. Even more important, I needed someone to take over mentally and emotionally for a little while. Two problem-solvers are better than one. When I learned to ask for help—especially when I was at my weakest physically and emotionally—I found others around me stepped up and, ultimately, that we became a powerful team. Never be afraid to reach out if you are struggling. There is help and hope, even if it doesn't always feel like it.

Embrace the differences

Embrace that you and your partner may parent differently. You have probably always done a lot of things differently; your differences just haven't been quite so in-your-face as they soon will be. You'll be trying to team up and create consistency for your little one, and your ideas about the best way to do that will be different some (or most) of the time. You may like different bottles; you may think certain toys

are better than others. You may even have a different way of
discussing which bottles or toys are the best!

For example, I'm a talker. I could hash out my thoughts
about child-rearing verbally all day long. My husband
hates doing that. He would rather think on his own about
it and then have a short session during which we try to
problem-solve. I save the hashing out for my girlfriends
(and my pediatrician), and I keep it short and sweet with
my hubby.

Recognize the strengths and weaknesses

Parenting is a balance of tasks and responsibilities, and one
partner may have more skills or patience for some of them.
My spouse is wonderful at taking the reins with our toddler.
He can make a 3-course dinner with grace. He can hold and
change the baby deftly during the day. But at night, especially once he went back to work, asking him to fully participate equally was like asking a slumbering bear to rouse
himself from his cave in the middle of winter.

What were the choices I felt I had at the beginning? Yell
at him (over and over) to please wake up or do it all myself.
To be honest, both made me resentful. Instead, I settled on a
more strengths-based plan: if he could just get her out of the
bassinet and change her the first few times she woke (plus,
obviously, stay up and problem-solve with me when we had
a rough night), I would handle the rest of the night shift. In
the day, he could do a little more baby holding while I rested
and breastfed.

Why did it take me until my second child arrived to realize
this was a more workable and, in the end, satisfying plan?
Because the first time around, I was way too focused on pre-
cise equality and task sharing, not considering that he would

happily take the lead during the day if I would just let the man sleep a little more at night.

Instead of evaluating or comparing contributions, figure out your partner's parenting superpowers. All of us bring amazing things to our parenting partnerships. I see all kinds of parents in clinic—analytical types asking tons of specific questions, the research-focused contingent searching for the evidence behind pediatric recommendations, and laid-back parents letting the stresses of early parenting easily roll off their backs. We all have something we bring to the table.

Your partner may be great at problem-solving sleep issues, while you are the baby bath master. If you divide and conquer according to the things you're naturally good at, you'll be a stronger team.

Encourage your partner's involvement from the beginning

I feel bad for modern-day dads like the one who lives in my house. But not as bad as I feel for modern-day moms. It seems when we empowered women to be just as fierce in the workplace as at home, forever changing modern-day mother-hood, we forgot about educating men on how to change their perspective on modern-day fatherhood. We figured they would just adjust without any effort or preparation, mag-ically skilled and knowledgeable in all things baby. Add in the Mr. Mom monikers and the media depictions of helpless dads fumbling through parenting—it's a not a surprise a lot of dads I see aren't sure exactly where they fit into the new parenting paradigm.

I know some amazing dads. My husband is one of them. He cares so much about teaching my kids about their worlds.

He's great at getting them excited about cooking and sports and gardening. He gets an A+ in my book (most days).

But the day my daughter came home, and he first earned his dad badge, he said he felt unprepared. Sure, we'd both been present at our birthing class and we both had learned how to swaddle a baby.

Looking back, though, he said he felt as if he didn't know what to expect when it came to typical baby behavior and definitely didn't feel ready to take the lead on newborn care. I'm sure it didn't help that his wife is a pediatrician. He assumed I would know it all when it came to raising a baby and thought I would want to take the lead on baby care. Still, the more dads I meet, the more I find so many feel the same way.

How do we include dads in the early baby care process? How do we, as moms-to-be, encourage and empower them to be equal players as we parent our young children?

Get educated together

How do people become experts in their fields? They study. If you are the only one in your family studying up on babies and parenting before or after your newborn arrives, you may feel as if you are the only one who knows anything, and you may be the only one who feels confident enough to take charge.

Everyone learns in different ways. If you learn best by reading, your partner may learn best by attending a class. Or, your partner may learn best by talking with other dads who have been through it. It probably won't work to force your partner to learn the exact same way you do, but expect that both of you have a working knowledge of common baby issues, newborn care basics, and proven calming techniques so that you can problem-solve from the same educated perspective.

Take a giant step back

For many people, it's annoying to have someone looking over your shoulder, micromanaging your every move. If you've ever had a super-controlling boss or are the child of a nit-picky parent, you know the feeling. When someone doesn't trust us or tries to manage us, it can make us feel resentful and irritated. We sometimes even lose our organic interest in the topic and stop putting our best effort into it.

That's what happens when we don't allow our partners to play an equal role in taking care of our children. We sabotage our hope of true co-parenting. Instead, be conscious about how to empower your other half to be the parenting boss more often. That might mean leaving the house so that your partner has the space to parent without your eagle eye. It definitely will mean holding your tongue (or sighs, or eye rolls, or judgment) if your partner is not doing things exactly how you would do them. If you both get educated together, you can be equal "experts" and this won't be so hard.

Give some respect

Dads are not complete duds in the baby care department, despite how most TV shows and movies depict them. Sometimes, we carry that same attitude toward our partners in real life. We may act like because our partners didn't birth our babies, they can't ever be bona fide baby whisperers.

The truth is, if we don't allow dads and other partners the space to be amazing family contributors, not just as winners at the office but also as dust-mop wielding, dinner-preparing, diaper-changing Jedis, we miss out on a ton of help and on a ton of balance in our lives. Your partner might not do things the same way you do them, but partners need their experiences with their child too. They are learning what feels most comfortable to them as well. And if this gives mom time to rest, then she should enjoy it.

Learn to say, "I'm sorry"

You are going through one of the most significant changes in your life. So is your partner. There will be times you will implode or explode from the stress of that transition. At times like these, figure out whether there is something to be learned or the pot of water just got a little too hot and boiled over.

When my daughter was 9 months old, we were driving home from a holiday gathering out of town and there was a huge traffic jam that set my daughter's bedtime back an hour and left her screaming in her car safety seat while we waited 15 minutes to reach the exit so that we could safely pull over. It wasn't a big deal, but because I was on day 3 of sleep training and I knew it would be harder for her to fall asleep at home because she was so overtired, it set me off.

I apologized to my husband later that night for convicting him of choosing the "wrong way home" and "ruining sleep training." Of course, it was not his fault. In fact, it had nothing to do with him. I was just aggravated at the situation. A crying child can cause stress to any situation and it's important to recognize that.

Find the core issue

Most of the time, arguments in the early parenting days will be a combination of fear—that something will happen to your baby, that you will never be "you" again, and that your baby isn't as advanced as other babies—frustration, and fatigue. It makes sense to develop a plan for self-care and for your relationship ahead of time so that you're not both caught off guard when things seem a little rocky. Having a new baby can be rough on relationships when you're first starting out, but it can also be an awesome opportunity to build teamwork, to clock memorable moments, and to appreciate what the other person brings to the table when it comes to parenting.

Accept help when it's offered

People always tell you when you have a new baby to get a lot of help. They tell you to take breaks, take turns with your partner, and let others cook and clean for you. It's great advice except that accepting help all the time often means a house full of well-meaning people giving unsolicited advice and observations for about 3 weeks while you hold a fussy baby and try not to lose it completely. I see the same situation with many of the new parents who come see me in my clinic.

One mom who comes to my practice had a particularly rowdy house just a few days after her baby was born. Her parents, sister's family, and parents-in-law all descended on her home from out of town. Every bed was filled and they even blew up air mattresses to accommodate the crowd. When her newborn cried in the middle of the night, she felt anxious the cries would wake her guests. As a result, she and her partner slept even more poorly than they would have if they had been solo.

The mom felt obligated to make sure everyone was well-fed. Her partner cooked breakfast for the group. They all sat through an extended meal while the baby fussed. Breastfeeding in her living room felt awkward, so she retreated to her bedroom alone throughout the day. After a day of entertaining, she craved privacy.

"If I were to do it again," she said, *"I would have asked my family to space out their visits. I also would have asked them to start coming a week later."*

In the beginning, caring for a new baby at home can be overwhelming. You are trying to figure things out as a new parent and trying to get your newborn onto a schedule. Perhaps a potentially better plan might be to let family and friends come in smaller spurts. Order takeout instead of having people cook every meal for you, or, sometimes, have them drop off food to enjoy later as a family.

Meaningful help might come from sources that seem less traditional, such as a doula or a caregiver. We relied pretty heavily on our nanny when we had our second baby. She was someone I knew would be respectful of our family process, would provide continuity for our eldest, and would not stress out easily. It's not that your loved ones are not important; it's that sometimes there is an extra layer of complexity to their constant involvement early on.

Set family boundaries

Are you an extrovert? Will it make you depressed not to have a posse around you at all times? Great. Let 'em help. But if not, let the newborn period be your first lesson in exercising parenting boundaries: do what will work the best for you and your family, even if it doesn't please every single person you know. You and your partner need to feel comfortable with whatever plan you decide on together.

Prioritize yourself

I remember a mommy friend telling me she had booked a day with a massage and a pedicure for herself a month after her second daughter arrived, and I felt slightly annoyed. She said she needed it. Really? What a seemingly selfish thing to do. But, in reality, she was doing herself and her family a huge favor. Taking small chunks of time for yourself as early on as possible is one of the best ways to keep yourself from feeling trapped as a new parent. Keeping yourself happy and healthy will allow you to give the best care possible to your new baby. You forget that you need a mental break sometimes to recharge your battery.

Make a self-care plan

The reality is, the only way to take the best care of your family is to make sure you're taking time to take care of yourself. Can you push through and be a mommy martyr for the next 18 years? Sure. Will it leave you resentful and angry? Most definitely.

Even though self-help is necessary, it's helpful to remember one simple principle: *you cannot have it all as a new mom.*

I know the media tells you otherwise. I know it seems like you *should* be having it all. But look at your life. Do you have it all now? Even when you've tried your best at it? Even without kids? I didn't.

I could never look exactly the way I wanted *and* be the best at my job *and* always have a hopping social calendar *and* travel the world *and* have tons of money in the bank *and* be peaceful and happy all the time at the same time. Anyone who tries to sell you otherwise is selling you lies.

You do, though, have time for the top 3 priorities in your life that are unique to you and your growing family. And if you choose things that really do fit your needs (as opposed to what other people want you to do), you will have more space for the extras.

My friend Christie is a business executive coach. She spends all day guiding leaders personally and professionally as they make million-dollar decisions. One night, discussing life at a bar, she took a cocktail napkin and wrote out the major categories of life—kids, spouse, work, exercise, friendships, hobbies, homemaking, travel and experiences, and appearance. For clarification, exercise to me meant releasing endorphins, stress reduction, and meditation, whereas appearance included everything that goes into looking put together (including exercise for the purpose of having a good appearance).

She wrote them in random order and then asked me to rank them in order in the left-hand column according to what I, in an ideal world, would spend the most time doing. "Rank them as a private, honest list, not based at all on what other people would think is the right way to rank them," she said.

I called it my *ideal list.*

IDEAL LIST

1. Exercise and stress reduction

2. Kids

3. Travel and experiences

4. Hobbies and sports (including writing and reading)

5. Partner

6. Friendships

7. Homemaking (tasks such as laundry and dishes)

8. Appearance

9. Work

In the next column, she asked me to rank what I thought I spent my time on.

Here is my *reality list.*

REALITY LIST

1. Work

2. Homemaking

3. Kids

4. Hobbies and sports

5. Partner

6. Appearance

7. Friendships

8. Exercise and stress reduction

9. Travel and experiences

Then, she told me to compare them.

My Comparison List of Major Life Categories— Side by Side	
Ideal	Reality
1. Exercise and stress reduction	1. Work
2. Kids	2. Homemaking
3. Travel and experiences	3. Kids
4. Hobbies	4. Hobbies
5. Partner	5. Partner
6. Friendships	6. Appearance
7. Homemaking	7. Friendships
8. Appearance	8. Exercise and stress reduction
9. Work	9. Travel and experiences

Look at the striking comparison between what my ideal life looked like and what my actual life looked like. This exercise is what convinced me to make a change in my life. Also, notice that while my kids ranked high on the list, they were not first. That's OK. In fact, it's probably healthier. Because, in the end, my kids are going to grow up and do their own thing (yours will too). My husband was also not first. That's OK too. It's important we have separate interests and desires, which we can build only if we spend some time doing things separately.

You might be thinking, "I'm going to have to work!" That is true for me too. That's how I pay for all the music classes, the nanny, and the nutritious quality food I want to provide for my kids in the first place. It's how my daughter goes to that fun preschool the nanny drops her off at. It's how we make sure we get to live in the house we do and get our kids into the great school district that they will eventually go to. There is not going to be some overhaul of my life that allows me to live work-free and spend all day sipping lattes while I supervise my children.

Also, you might have a different top 3 than I do, and that is totally fine. My husband is a huge extrovert. I had him make this list, and his was in a completely different order. No problem. That's the beauty of it.

I'm not saying don't go to work or don't figure out a way to get your house clean once your newborn arrives, but, as my friend says, "Work is like a parasite. It will leach out of you as much as you will give to it." Same with housecleaning and coordinating 80 million schedules. Of course, we have to do some of that to keep things running smoothly, but we can't let them suck the life out of us. The rest of the things on the list you'll have to consider like gravy or a cherry on top if you can get to them, at least in the early weeks and months of motherhood. It's OK if your makeup isn't perfect, your socks aren't organized, and you can't remember the last time you cooked something more complicated than a quesadilla.

Sounds good to get your priorities in line from the get-go, right? But it takes a little preplanning to make it happen. I learned early on that to do all I do, I have to automate and delegate.

Automate and delegate

Here is a simple truth: you are not the only person who can take care of your home, your kids, your bills, or your calendar. A ton of information is out there about mental overload and what it is doing, particularly to women, to have constant running lists of to-dos in our minds all day long.

The following aspects are some examples of how I've automated and delegated that changed my life. Of course, everyone is in a different position in budget. I'm not trying to make you go into debt. But, if it is at all possible, here are some changes I made so that I stopped drowning in chores.

Hire a house cleaner

I'm not sure what took me so long to get a house cleaner. But I will say, my family consistently insinuates that it is not my best skill, so I should have known I was spinning my wheels when I tried over and over to clean like a pro. Hiring a house cleaner did 2 things for me: it forced me to organize my house the night before she came over (eg, put away all the clothes, pick up around the house), and it made me feel extremely calm as I stopped looking around my house every minute, feeling guilty and wishing it was more together as I tried to corral 2 small children.

Find or hire someone, even if it's a neighbor kid, to mow your lawn. Even the National Academy of Sciences agrees with me on this one. *The New York Times* and *Travel and Leisure* both published articles about the science-backed advantage of letting others do some of your dirty work.

Learn to automate

Look into options that can make life easier. Prepackaged meal kits available through online subscriptions or at the grocery store can offer delicious meals that are easy to make or are ready to bake. Pay attention to salt content and the actual amounts of fruits and vegetables (not all are created equal). I'm a fan of online meal plans that are plant based and can be adjusted to vegetarian lifestyles, that have a family plan, and that allow you to skip weekly delivery whenever you want. I have an app on my phone, and they send me reminders each week to pick meals. We use this service for 3 of our meals per week, make simple dinners such as chicken with broccoli and a grain 2 times a week, and then feel less guilty when we occasionally order takeout.

Take advantage of technology

I use online shopping for *everything*. Diapers, wipes, sippy cups, and household items such as paper towels, hand soap, and toilet paper. I love retail stores like the next mom, but I do *not* want to drag my kids through a store every other week. I also do not want to spend my time in a grocery store for basics. It's fun to pick out something to add to our family meals or to get specialty items, but carrying around a list and hauling 2 little people around can be exhausting.

Instead, I order groceries online every week and have them delivered to my home in 2 hours or at a scheduled day and time. By ordering from the same sites over and over and paying a yearly fee, I get free shipping, which takes the pressure off if I happen to forget an item after I virtually check out. I use my online shopping cart as a running grocery list throughout the week, adding dish soap and batteries as I realize I need them. When it's time to make my weekly order, I've already accounted for items that would have otherwise fallen off my radar.

Get smart about bills

What bills do you not have on automatic pay? What monthly or weekly items do you constantly forget? Do you have a system to remind yourself of to-dos as they come up for you randomly? Look on company websites for directions on setting up automatic pay so that your bills are constantly paid on time. Online banking can save you time and help get your finances in order.

Shop for clothing online

Children's clothing is another area in which it pays to use technology. I focus on quality basics that can be handed down kid to kid, when possible. I would rather spend a little more but have to shop only 4 times a year (with some fun "Let's get a special outfit" outings sprinkled in) than pay less per item and have it last less than a month. This is very budget dependent, but, especially if you have multiple kids and they are the same gender, buying quality over quantity can make a difference.

Seasonal sales can also be a busy mom's lifesaver. Most major brands slash prices on inventory at least every 6 months. Take advantage of major sales to stock up on clothes for the following year. You may not be able to predict precisely what size your child will be 12 months from the time you make your purchase, but, for the major savings, it's worth it to go ahead and make an educated guess. After just a few washes, most kid clothes will start to shrink anyway, making exact sizing less relevant.

Multitask or simplify

Use the car to your full advantage

If you have a newborn and are breastfeeding, this is one of the most important, time-saving tricks around. I used it with both of my children. While parked (safety first!) in my car, I used a hands-free pumping bra to make my outings efficient. Inserting the breast shields into the bra and attaching my hands-free pump, I covered myself with a breastfeeding cover, turned the pump on, and drove wherever I needed to go. On the way to exercise class and on the way in between meetings, it made my car the perfect pumping station. And it was, obviously, hands-free.

I used a cooler pack, and disposable cleaning wipes made specifically for breast pump parts were great for short trips when I didn't have access to a sink. Then I thoroughly washed and sterilized everything once I was home or at work.

Maximize nap time

Your baby's naps are a great time for you to rest. Yes, they can also be a time to do the dishes and put a load of laundry in, but once your baby arrives and you're in the swing of things, take stock of how you feel at the end of nap times. My guess is, if you spend the whole time breathlessly taking care of tasks, you'll feel exhausted. Consider dividing out what you do during naps so that you complete 1 or 2 tasks such as doing the dishes and doing one load of laundry.

Then take some time to regroup and do something you want to do (even if it is scrolling through social media feeds) so that you're not wishing you were doing that when your little one wakes up.

Same goes for planning. Set a planning day every week. My day is Wednesday. I like to get all organized Wednesday nights so that I can spend Thursdays with my girls. It's the night I look at the calendar and I figure out meals for the week, look through my mail pile, shop online for household basics, check my checking accounts, and hash out details about upcoming events I have with my husband.

Use audiobooks and podcasts

On days I am driving to work or running errands, I spend the time in the car listening to podcasts and audiobooks. I love reading paperback books, but I just know I would never have the time to get to everything I've had on my "meaning to" list if I relied on my evenings and weekends to do those things. That was especially true when I became a new mom. The car became a place where when I was by myself, I knew I could get a lot done by listening. As a new mom, you are always doing things for others in your family, so be good to yourself and treat yourself when you can.

Get organized

Last, find the system of organization that fits you. I still use an old-school notebook to write out my goals and to project plan, but I need my phone calendar to keep organized. If something is not in my calendar, it does not exist. Whatever the tool, find something you know you will use and can rely on to keep you scheduled and on track.

Find a self-care ritual

Start with exercise

If there was going to be a single activity that is worth time by yourself and for yourself, physical fitness (if you choose the right activity—anything with an endorphin release) or meditation takes the cake. Physical fitness can give you the chance to deepen your social connections, be mindful, work on your own physical fitness, and set goals for yourself. Meditation also checks many of those same boxes, but there is something valuable in moving our bodies as a way to clear the mental and physical cobwebs away.

This is not about being a size 2 or fitting into your favorite jeans (although, obviously, if you're working out consistently, you're also likely going to reap the physical benefits, including cardiovascular health and weight maintenance). As moms, we definitely don't need more societal pressure to be perfectly thin or polished, but if you are taking better care of your body and feeling better about how you look and feel day to day, that confidence is going to spill over into everything else you do.

Decide on a plan that works for you

Choose a routine that works for you, not that fits others' expectations or sounds good to your friends or family. This is not about them; it's 180% about you.

When I was choosing an exercise program for myself postpartum, my friends and my husband talked a lot about running, Pilates, or joining a gym. Those can be *great* for some people. I have done a lot of running in the past, and it was amazing, but I didn't feel it was the right thing for me this time around.

They also suggested working out first thing in the morning. "Get up really early, go work out, get ready, and then go straight to work," they said.

I tried that for a long time, feeling as if that was the most responsible path to take, the way that would least inconvenience everyone else around me. But it didn't work for 3 reasons.

1. **I never worked as hard as I would later in the day when I went to morning classes.** I felt sorry for myself that I was up so early and didn't push myself because I was proud of myself just for showing up.

2. **I hardly ever actually went.** I always found an excuse, namely, sleeping in as much as possible, but also kids waking up early needing my attention, work meetings, and illness—you name it, I used it as an excuse.

3. **I was exhausted by the time I finished exercising, getting ready for the day, and getting myself to my job.** I'm sure you can guess how often I worked out. That's right: never. Nope. Self-care is just like birth control. The type of birth control that is best for you is the one you will use consistently. The type of self-care you choose is the kind that fits you and your desires and life.

Instead, I took classes directly after work when I needed the most stress relief. I changed before leaving the office and drove straight to the exercise studio. That way, I didn't lose motivation and was already dressed by the time class started at 6:00 pm.

Almost hilariously, now running and 6:00 am workouts are the mainstay of my exercise and self-care regimen. That's because I have children who sleep through the night consistently and I have a lot of early evening work commitments. I try to go to bed by 9:30 pm so that I get a full night's rest by the time I wake up in the morning at 5:30 am. I sign up for exercise classes on my studio's app. They have a strict cancellation policy, making it impossible to cancel past 10:00 pm the night before without paying a fine. The threat of a $15 penalty motivates me to show up on time.

Most important, I've learned to give myself some grace. I'm much more concerned with getting some type of physical fitness in consistently than with making sure I work my absolute hardest during every workout session. A different season in my life equals a different self-care approach.

Pay attention to new mom exercise and self-care considerations

If you're a new mom reading this chapter, you may be raring to get back to your "pre-baby" exercise routine. Take a second to make sure you're safe as you get started. Most moms are shocked by the hormonal shifts they experience postpartum and many feel discouraged when they look in the mirror right after their babies arrive. It can be difficult to stop looking back at the previous, pre-baby physical version of yourself wistfully instead of looking forward to life as the new postpartum you, adjusting your expectations accordingly. You'll want to think specifically about these health factors as you start out on your postpartum exercise (and self-care) journey. Check with your health care professional about your individual needs.

PELVIC FLOOR DYSFUNCTION

It is not normal to pee every time you run or every time you cough. It's also not normal in our society to talk about the fact that you do. If you had a knee surgery, you would automatically plan on rehabilitating that knee after your procedure. Somehow, though, we put women's pelvic floor health into a separate, hush-hush category. We shouldn't. Urinary incontinence is exceedingly common among postpartum patients who deliver vaginally—but *nobody* talks about it.

I probably had a small amount of pelvic floor dysfunction after my first baby, but it wasn't until 2 years after my second baby came into the world that I actually realized just how bad it was. When I started running more, I found myself (blush) peeing my pants. Most of the time it happened at the end of my longer runs when my muscles were fatigued. Sometimes, it was more than just a little bit. It took a couple months for me to motivate myself to get a pelvic floor physical therapy evaluation because, well, I was in a bit of denial. After just one session, though, I wished I had gone sooner.

DIASTASIS RECTI

Remember, your body (especially your core) just went through a major transition. Check with your health care professional to see whether you have diastasis recti (a separation in the abdominal wall muscles) or you need to just strengthen your abdominal muscles. This is important because, for one, if you have either of these problems, you're going to look pregnant for a longer time after you deliver. And, even if you go hard-core with traditional abdominal exercises such as crunches without addressing diastasis recti first, it can make that prolonged postpartum abdomen appearance even worse. Plus, weak core muscles can contribute to problems such as poor posture and back pain.

Most moms can start exercise at about the 6- to 8-week mark once cleared by a doctor, but take care to not overdo it. Your body is still recovering well after you give birth.

POSTPARTUM DEPRESSION AND ANXIETY

Seek care early if you're feeling sad or worried. About 1 in 9 women experiences postpartum depression, a serious disorder that's often not detected until symptoms become severe. When I started exercising postpartum—especially doing deeper, reflective activities such as yoga—a lot of surprising feelings of loss came up for me. Not only was my body not the same, my emotions also felt foreign. I'm glad I told my doctor and my family how I was feeling so that I could get the help I needed. It's not a sign of weakness to admit things aren't going well—it's a sign of strength!

Almost 80% of women experience mild unhappiness or worry in the postpartum period, but those low-level baby blues typically last only a few days to weeks. New moms with postpartum depression and anxiety, on the other hand, have much more severe symptoms. They can develop extreme sadness or hopelessness, as well as physical symptoms such as difficulty sleeping, eating, or concentrating. Often, affected mothers have a hard time bonding with their babies and in extreme cases can even consider harming their babies. Women need their partners to be watch guards for this debilitating disease, but often, social stigma and lack of information keep a mom and her circle of support ignorant until it's too late.

When partners recognize a problem developing, they can seek help from a mental health professional, encourage moms to practice self-care, and start to strengthen their own bonds with their babies by assuming an (at least) equal role in care.

To break the stigma around postpartum depression and anxiety, we have to educate moms-to-be and their families about perinatal mental health and address head-on the social and policy factors that contribute to this epidemic. Most important, we have to give pregnant women realistic information about caring for their babies and themselves before their babies ever arrive.

Find a schedule that fits your life

As you develop a self-care plan, you'll also have to decide how much time you're willing or able to commit to weekly. I decided pretty early on that 3 days a week was a reasonable goal.

What is something you can do 3 days a week, almost every single week? Of course, you will have setbacks, but if you can commit to 3 times a week most weeks, it will be often enough that you stick with it and it will become a routine. If you can get to your activity more often, awesome, but 3 times a week is a great start.

I schedule my self-care this way.

1. One weekend morning

2. One weekday evening when my husband is with our kids

3. One weekday evening when a caregiver is with our kids

Take advantage of everyday moments

You might be thinking that leaving your newborn will be impossible 3 times a week. In the beginning, especially as a breastfeeding mom, self-care will likely come in more abbreviated, sporadic moments. It may be something small, such as taking 5 minutes to listen to your favorite song with your eyes closed, getting a small treat (lattes are my vice), going outside, or simply taking 10 big breaths. Or it may be bigger, such as taking 30 minutes to an hour to read a book or going to the grocery store alone. Even now, on my 4 undedicated self-care days, I make sure that I get at least 5 purposeful minutes to myself.

Pay attention to your breathing

You'll have to breathe anyway. How will you do it? Will you hold your breath? Take small breaths over and over? Can you learn how to concentrate on your breathing a little more when you get stressed? Even the way you move air in or out will contribute to your sense of peace and mindfulness as a new mom.

Choose to enjoy

I've talked about taking advantage of naps and time in the car, but sometimes it pays just to enjoy instead of multitask.

Once I returned from my maternity leave, I made it a point *not* to listen to the news on the way home from work. Instead, I used that time to turn on loud music and enjoy it. I saved my news and podcast consumption for errands and my work commute.

At home, when my kids were asleep, we were intentional in the early days to watch a lot of comedies and to listen to a lot of frivolously entertaining audiobooks.

Take a break

Take the time—even if it's 5 to 10 minutes—to get your head right in the middle of the day. If you're at home, it might be in the shower when you get a second to relax or at a time when your baby is asleep. If you are returning to work, it might be a moment at lunch when you turn off your phone, shut down your computer, and take a second to yourself or with your colleagues.

Make mommy friends

Motherhood was never meant to be attempted alone, yet in the United States, isolated "mommy-ing" is a common approach. Even before we have children, we often make more connections daily via social media than we do face-to-face with our peers. But when it comes to being a new mom, you need an actual, in-person village. Support may come from close friends, other moms you meet along the way, or family members. Even if you're naturally private, this is a time you'll need the insight and experience others have to offer.

Every mom is different when it comes to making connections and finding support. Hospital-sponsored "baby and me" classes, during which you sit in a circle and share your parenting questions and experiences with other new parents, are places where deep bonds can develop because you and the other participants all share a unique vulnerability as you try to navigate the complexities of caring for a baby.

Activity-based community opportunities such as baby and me music classes or hiking groups are also good ways to find like-minded parents.

Give your partner space

Remember, your partner needs time to regroup too! Don't be stingy with taking care of yourself or with allowing the other caregivers in your life the chance to do the same. Before the birth, brainstorm activities that will bring your partner joy postpartum, either with you or as an individual.

Brian is a first-time dad who loves golf. Before his baby was born, he spent time on the link at least 3 times a month. Brian wasn't a country club member; he just enjoyed hitting balls on a community course with friends after work. The fresh air and casual banter with his buddies relaxed him after a long day at the office.

In the first few months of parenthood, Brian felt guilty leaving his family intermittently to pursue his hobby. It felt frivolous, especially because he knew his baby was particularly colicky in the evenings when he usually met up with friends to golf pre-baby. He supported his wife's self-care efforts, but he felt bad about taking care of his own needs and enjoyment. After a while, he said he felt more and more dissatisfied with his new day-to-day existence as a dad.

Brian and his wife had a weekly rhythm that worked for them as a couple before they had kids. Once the baby came, it seemed to all go away. His wife was stressed and he was stressed too. Even though he understood it wasn't realistic to expect everything to be the same now that their newborn was here, he still needed a few moments to himself.

When Brian finally figured out a way to make that happen (such as adjusting his work schedule slightly to accommodate some early evening putting sessions and making sure he and his wife spoke openly when they were overwhelmed), the whole family was a lot happier. Over time, Brian said he felt as if he was able to be a more present, relaxed father and partner just by carving out a few self-care hours per week.

Keep your brain active

Experienced parents set up a plan for what to do with their time once their baby arrives. They focus on keeping their brains active starting at week 1.

I spent so much time postpartum as a new mom sitting and watching TV. Alone. With my baby sleeping on me. It sounds cute and it was, for a few days. But, in the end, it was a bad thing to be isolated and mindless for so long.

When baby number 2 came along, I made a commitment to turn off the TV and turn on background music instead. I made playlists so that I could already have music on command that inspired and relaxed or energized me. I set up some (very light) contract work to do for a local health organization during my maternity leave. Mental engagement that is not stressful and not baby related is so important for newbie moms, especially if they are used to being at work 40 hours per week.

Store breast milk

As soon as your milk "comes in," use it to your advantage. Store small amounts so that you can take small breaks starting at week 3 to 4. In the beginning, you will have way more milk than you will once you are back to work pumping. It won't derail your breastfeeding efforts to pump some of that and put it into the freezer or refrigerator. Here's how to do it: feed your baby first, then pump a little off to store—maybe 1 or 2 times per day.

If you are having supply issues to begin with, *of course,* give whatever your baby needs to him first. Also, if you are having overproduction issues and a lactation specialist tells you to do block feeding (feeding from only one breast during a breastfeeding session), pump off only enough to handle discomfort issues. But if that is not you, earn your freedom faster by pumping that milk and letting others share that bonding time with the newborn by feeding him with a bottle. Make sure your latch and milk supply are established—at about 3 to 4 weeks.

Plan ahead when you are trying to wean

Oftentimes, when you are weaning your baby, you'll have a bit of engorgement because your body is confused. Particularly if you have been breastfeeding your baby for a long time, your body will automatically be ready to feed your baby at a session time you may have decided to cut out.

This is especially true in the morning. Although you don't want to give your body the full message "Yes! This body is still open for business!" you want to relieve some of the discomfort from weaning engorgement. A hand pump can be great for this. A double-electric pump can also work, but it takes longer to set up in the middle of the night or in the morning.

The great news is that a hand pump is cheap compared with the cost of a double-electric breast pump; a hand pump will typically cost $18 to $34. It does *not* replace the double-electric pump, though. If you are trying to maintain

Human Milk Storage Guidelines			
	Storage Location and Temperatures		
Type of Breast Milk	Countertop 77°F (25°C) or colder (room temperature)	Refrigerator 40°F (4°C)	Freezer 0°F (−18°C) or colder
Freshly Expressed or Pumped	Up to **4 Hours**	Up to **4 Days**	Within **6 months** is best Up to **12 months** is acceptable
Thawed, Previously Frozen	1–2 Hours	Up to **1 Day** (24 hours)	NEVER refreeze human milk after it has been thawed
Leftover from a Feeding (baby did not finish the bottle)	Use within **2 hours** after the baby is finished feeding		

Reproduced from Division of Nutrition, Physical Activity, and Obesity; National Center for Chronic Disease Prevention and Health Promotion. Proper storage and preparation of breast milk. Centers for Disease Control and Prevention website. https://www.cdc.gov/breastfeeding/recommendations/handling_breastmilk.htm. Reviewed August 6, 2019. Accessed October 4, 2019.

your milk supply, only a baby sucking at your breast or using a double-electric pump will do the trick, because both create significantly more sustained suction for a longer period of time.

Consider purchasing a breast pump that works with the rest of your breast pump system. Several companies make similar products that integrate with their respective bottles and pump parts. The downside is that you have to manually pump the breast to get the milk flowing.

CHAPTER 5

Finding a Child Care Provider

So you want to find an amazing child care provider? I get it. I did too. Kind of desperately. Like in an "I am really trying to not bawl right now at the thought of leaving my precious baby in the arms of someone else, so if that someone else could be dreamlike, it would really help" kind of way. Choosing a child care provider is one of the most important choices you make for your kids early on. The people your children are around strongly influence the way they see the world and the place they find within it.

I'm not going to mince words here. I have the world's best nanny. She has been with me for 4 years, through 2 very different infants, a house remodel, and too many kid viruses to mention. You name the task, she has done it. She makes my world go round, and she's gracious enough not to let it go to her head.

I'm assuming you want to find an amazing child care provider too. I get it and, the good news is, I don't have the world's best nanny by luck. I have her by design. I had a specific plan when I set out to find her. So when parents ask me for recommendations on this topic, I have plenty of advice.

First and foremost, parents ask me often about what type of setting is best for children—child care, family care, or in-home nanny care. My answer is never black-and-white because, like almost all things in life, it depends. I care most about quality, and in my book, quality child care provides a safe space where kids can build deep, one-on-one connections with their caregivers and peers and is a place where kids do not get sick all day, every day (very important for all working parents). The program or person also needs to provide the level of flexibility you need. Finally, you want the adults caring for your child to have the same parenting goals and values you do, backed by a working knowledge of the core principles of successful caregiving.

You don't want them to try too hard to focus on a set "curriculum" for your children. Instead, you want them to provide opportunities for exposure to lots of books, music, one-on-one communication, and exploration. This could be in the care of a child care center, an in-home child care setting, a nanny, a nanny share, a friend, or a relative.

My top picks are nannies, family members, and in-home child care settings for young kids. Once kids reach preschool age, the need for structure and social skill development outweighs the home care aspect. At that point, a mix of preschool and sitter/nanny is my top choice. Of course, budget often comes into play, and traditional child care settings with quality, reliable caregivers are a great option too.

Child Care

When you set out to find a child care center, start by talking with other parents in your area. Chances are seasoned parents will start recommending child care centers once their own kids are ready to start the next level of school in the fall. Depending on your location, you may need to get onto waiting lists *early* (eg, as soon as you're pregnant; I know, we live in a competitive world). It's never too soon to start researching.

Look for child care centers that share these goals for your kids, giving care in a way that helps kids.

- Contribute to society.
- Find contentment in their work and play.
- Form healthy relationships.
- Build resilience.

Consider the possibility of increased risk of illness. A child in child care will be exposed to more germs daily than a child in a one-on-one or nanny share setting just because of the sheer number of other children she's around. Yes, over time that can contribute to a stronger immune system, but, for some families, it can mean a world of hurt every winter. Every child is different—some kids seem to skate by without a cold or rash—but it is a recurring theme.

Even though a nanny or smaller in-home setting can seem more expensive on the surface, your cost-benefit child care analysis should also account for potential days of work missed caused by your child's illnesses if he'll be in a group care setting. In my profession, it's not impossible to take a day off, but it is a huge inconvenience to my patients and to my business partners. So that I can prevent missed workdays, I look for ways to prevent my kids catching major illnesses in the first place.

Nanny Care

Likely because I've had such a good child care experience personally, friends and patients ask me consistently where to find a good nanny.

The answer: there are a ton of places to look for quality caregiver suggestions—online caregiver search sites, friends, family, coworkers, social media groups, and even professional nanny companies. On the websites specifically designed for finding care, they'll make it easy for you to go through all the steps—they'll allow you to create a profile and a job posting where you then filter through applicants and set up in-person interviews. From there, you can sign up for a paid trial during which the caregiver cares for your child for just an hour or so while you're still in the house so that you can make sure you feel comfortable.

Here's the secret, though: it's not about where; it's about how. It doesn't matter what site you use or what friend makes an initial suggestion. It matters what process you go through to attract, evaluate, and hire potential candidates.

Here are my top 4 strategies for finding an amazing caregiver.

Focus on the details

Be thorough and specific as you outline your needs. Make sure you've covered all the things that really matter to you as you create your job description so that the standard of applicant is raised from the get-go and you don't attract people who aren't a good fit. This is my exact job posting when I was looking.

My husband and I are currently pregnant with our first baby and are due with our little girl mid-October. I will have about three months off work and then will go back. We are looking for a great nanny to care for our little one at our home on the days I work. We need someone sporadically starting in October and consistently starting in January. In mid-October to mid-January, it would be for babysitting, to get to know us and her, so I can get a break some days and so I could fill in at my work some days if needed before I officially go back.

We could work out what would work for your schedule, but we don't have specific guaranteed hours in mind. Starting mid-January, it would be part time guaranteed two days per week (the days I am working, which are Tuesday and Friday) plus whatever works for both parties for extra babysitting/extra days, etc. We're looking for someone who could for sure commit to working with us until our daughter is one but possibly for longer, depending on our needs plus your needs.

Stay serious

Present yourself in a way that attracts the person you want working for you. Get a contract together so that you look professional. Delineate vacation and sick day expectations, salary, work hours, and household duties. Online child care search sites such as Care.com (www.care.com) and Sittercity (www.sittercity.com) will often have free downloadable templates you can use as a jumping-off point. Refine your contract according to your individual needs.

Plan ahead

My nanny told me that when she saw my job posting, she was really impressed, because I posted it about 3 months before I had my baby. I didn't need regular care for 6 months from the time of the job posting. She said she loved that. However, if you are about to have your baby and you are just now trying to find care, please try to stay calm. All is not lost.

She explained to me, "If you are a really serious nanny and you're looking for a transition, you don't just try to find a position 2 weeks ahead of time. You look 4 to 6 months ahead."

Similarly, if you are searching for child care centers, expect high-demand sites to have long waiting lists. Start your search early if possible.

Be choosy

Feel free to weed out those who don't quite measure up. This is your kid we're talking about. You want a caregiver you feel great about. Filter out applicants who don't present themselves professionally (by having spelling or grammatical errors), who don't have the quality of experience you're looking for, or who don't fit your style. If you start your search early, you're more likely to allow enough time to find a good pool of applicants from which to choose.

Sometimes when you meet someone in person, it becomes even clearer that the person is right (or wrong) for you. Use your gut to make your final decision. Check references. When someone said, "I know this is a big deal and I can tell you without reservation that you will be so happy you chose her—she's like family at this point," I knew I had found a winner.

Stay real

Stay real about the things that really matter to you in a caregiver. Of course, things such as CPR (cardiopulmonary resuscitation)-certified status are important to me, but the 5 characteristics that topped my list once I got past my checkbox items were the following ones.

INTUITIVE

I wanted someone who was intuitive and confident. In my experience, this comes only from real experience. As a pediatrician, once you've seen a hundred ear infections, you can spot one a mile away. The same hard-earned confidence goes for caregivers.

If someone has "more than 10 years' experience" on her résumé but it means occasionally babysitting a neighbor, it doesn't count as much as someone who has cared for 4 families over the course of 5 to 10 years, ranging in ages from infancy to 15 years. People like that probably know their stuff.

TRUSTWORTHY

I wanted someone who was trustworthy. When we had our in-person interview with our nanny, I told her I was looking for someone who could call me for anything but who felt comfortable in most situations so that the person wouldn't need to unless there was a real emergency.

Turns out that was what our nanny was looking for too. She told me that one of the main reasons *she* chose *us* was because she knew she wouldn't be micromanaged all day long on things she knew a lot about. She presented herself as a professional and expected to be treated in the same way. She, of course, defers to my direction if needed, but because she is so trustworthy and confident, I hardly ever feel the need to redirect.

LOVING

I wanted someone who would deeply love my kids. I think sometimes this can be one of the most daunting aspects of this whole search, but the reality is, when you are searching for someone to care for your children regularly, it matters that they are loved during that time (of course, in a way that keeps your kids safe and that has appropriate boundaries), not just "watched."

You can never be completely sure how people will care for your child, but you can tell a lot from the way they talk about prior children they've cared for. When you ask potential caregivers about their prior experience, listen carefully. My nanny spoke warmly about each of her past jobs. I could tell the children she took care of were like family to her as I heard her thoughtfully recount some of her best memories with them. The way she described her experiences gave a clue as to the way she felt about each of those relationships. Her references verified that family vibe, specifically mentioning how they included her in special celebrations and sometimes even family vacations.

This takes a little bit of letting go. It means that your children will form a relationship with someone who is not you, that they might one day call your nanny "Mom" or "Dad" inadvertently, or that it may sometimes feel as if they love your nanny (*gulp!*) more than they love you. I feel your pain. Your children might very well come to love their caregiver, and that would be the *best-case* scenario, in the end. When I finally put aside my pride and didn't let that sabotage my nanny-search efforts, I was more successful.

KNOWLEDGEABLE

I wanted someone who had a solid understanding of child development. I knew that eventually, my nanny would be the one to discipline my kids during the day. At first, it would be all roses and sunshine while they were cute and cuddly, but if I was in this for the long haul (which I was), there would come a time she would be handling tantrums and time-outs. I wanted her to be comfortable with this and for it to be second nature to her.

Let me be clear: this doesn't mean a caregiver has to take official courses in child development. It also doesn't necessarily mean that a caregiver can quote experts in the field of behavioral management (can you?). It means that caregivers can walk you through what they would do if a tricky situation came up with your child, with the explanation making you say, "That is perfectly OK with me," or even, "Wow, I would never have thought to do that! That's a genius idea!"

A GOOD FIT

I wanted someone I actually liked. This is so important. You really have to make sure that the person you hire is someone you would be OK spending time with or, even better, would want to spend time with. Caregivers don't need to be your best friend, but odds are, you will develop a friendship with them as you share the responsibility of raising your kids together. If you are irritated by your caregiver half the time, the odds of this all working out will start to wear on you. Spend time in your interview asking a bit about your potential employee so that you have a good sense of the person you are inviting into your home.

Family and Friends

Friends and family can also be amazing pinch-hit caregivers or caregivers for extended trips. If you have an open, honest relationship with a family member you trust, that person can also work well as a full-time nanny. The obvious bonus? Free care (or at least significantly reduced cost). The downside? For many parents, establishing long-term care with a family member can be more complicated than a traditional child care arrangement because there is no formal employer-employee relationship. The best way to address this is to set up expectations for what your needs are and your kids' needs are and to let the chips fall where they may (as long as there are no major safety violations) if things aren't to your exact specifications.

Paid caregivers will also vary in their willingness or ability to meet your expectations, but it's a little easier when dealing with an employee because you are *paying employees*. If it doesn't work out, you can usually end or alter your relationship with significantly less dramatic fallout. If the caregiving prowess or style doesn't quite measure up, you can choose to find someone new without the emotional considerations that come with personal relationship negotiations. On the flip side, it can be difficult for friends and family to understand or respect your boundaries or your parenting style. Sometimes you have to make a hard decision—is it worth it financially to muddy the friend and family waters and if it is, will you be able to let go of the smaller things that irk you?

The Most Important Caregiver Consideration

Focus on finding experienced, quality providers. Like most things in life, what really matters when it comes to child care is that you feel comfortable and confident with your choice. The exact location or setup—child care, nanny care, or family care—matters less. Child care centers and nannies can be great options, but just make sure you find quality caregivers who share your goals and values—that is most important. Finding a nanny or caregiver can be stressful, but it's also very exciting. You're building your village; you're hiring the person who will be there for your kids alongside you, nurturing, guiding, and caring for the person or people you love best. You'll find amazing people waiting in the wings to work with you.

Nanny Sample Questionnaire

Experience
- Number of families you have nannied for and ages of children
- Length of time with other families
- Specific experience with newborns

Availability
- Current hours of availability
- Other commitments (eg, school, other families, part-time jobs)
- Upcoming vacation needs and anticipated time-off needs

Health
- Vaccination status
- Smoking and other substance use status

Certifications and Education
- CPR (cardiopulmonary resuscitation) and first aid certification status
- Child development knowledge and experience
- Comfort level with health issues (eg, fevers, colds, emergencies, special needs)

Favorite Ages and Activities With Kids
- Knowledge of local kid-friendly venues
- Favorite local parks, swimming pools, and classes

Handling Difficult Situations
- Describe a time a baby was crying uncontrollably and you had to figure out why.
- Describe a difficult situation you've had with a toddler and how you solved it.
- Describe an emergency you've had to deal with.

Negative or Positive Past Work Experiences
- Describe what went well or what was frustrating.
- Describe a "deal breaker" for you when finding a nanny position.

Additional Tasks
- Open to light housecleaning or cooking?
- Able to transport kids via car or public transportation?

Other Families and Hobbies
- Open to playdates with other children?
- Any special hobbies (eg, art, music, other languages you would incorporate into child care)?

Child Care Center Sample Questionnaire

Certifications
- Is the center licensed and accredited by the state?
- What level of education and what certifications does staff have?
- What ongoing trainings do you complete with staff about child development and behavioral management?

Finances
- What are the daily or monthly tuition rates?
- What's the financial policy for late pickup?
- How much does it cost to secure a spot on the waiting list?

Schedules
- What are the daily drop-off and pickup windows?
- What is the daily schedule, including naps?
- Are there preplanned holiday or vacation week closures throughout the year?

Behavior and Child Development
- What is your center's educational philosophy or care philosophy?
- How do you handle conflicts between children?
- How much time is spent outside? Is there a dedicated outdoor play area at the facility?
- Do you provide daily reports for kids' behaviors or activities?
- What are the expectations around potty training and diaper changes?

Staffing
- What is the staff turnover rate?
- How do you screen employees for hire?
- How many children are in each room and at the facility in total?
- What is the staff to child ratio at the facility?
- When do kids typically move up from an infant room to a toddler room or from a toddler room to a preschool room?

Feeding
- How do you handle frozen or pumped breast milk preparation or formula preparation?
- What is served for meals or snacks? Do parents need to provide food?

Child Care Center Sample Questionnaire
(continued)

Safety and Health
- What is the sick policy for children and for staff?
- How often and how do you sanitize the toys and materials at the center?
- What are the vaccination rates among children currently in the center?
- How do you keep your facility safe and secure?
- Do you ever transport children outside the facility? If so, how?

Parent Involvement
- Do you provide parent-child development education opportunities?
- What is the policy on parents visiting the child care center during the day?

CHAPTER 6

In the Hospital

Kelly was the first of her friends to have a baby. When she found out she was pregnant, her first emotion was pure elation. Every time she thought about being a mom, she became more and more excited.

As the big day drew nearer, though, a different kind of feeling took hold: trepidation. What would it be like to birth a baby? Would it be as painful and arduous as the media portrays it? Should she think through her birth plan beforehand?

As she researched on her own and heard from acquaintances about their birth processes, she wondered if there were hidden tricks to making her experience easier, ones they didn't teach you in prenatal classes. Social media certainly suggested there were. It seemed as if every mom who came before her had a tale to tell or an infographic to share on the internet. She scoured Pinterest for as much secret intel as she could find only to realize afterward that most of the guidance wasn't accurate or appropriate for her individual birth situation.

I'm not sure when Pinterest became the go-to information source for moms-to-be. It has simplified checklists for all things in the pregnancy and birth preparation realm, that's for sure. There are sample checklists for what to bring to the hospital, for how to pack for postpartum needs, and for what to include in your birth plan (the most successful moms I meet have a very simple birth plan of "keeping mom and baby healthy and safe," by the way).

I think the cultural obsession we have with planning and controlling the birth and postpartum period is rooted in fear. We're scared it will all go wrong. And we're a little bit right; sometimes it goes wrong. But usually, it goes just fine, and the superficial checklist items we make sure we address before baby comes are definitely not the deciding factors in our success. It will all be OK no matter what labor playlist you curate or which bathrobe you pack. It will work out no matter which newborn outfit you buy for the car ride home.

There are, though, factors that play a role in helping you and your baby get off on the right foot. The first is having a basic understanding of how the hospital system works and who the main players are in your care. Knowing this information can help you self-advocate effectively. The second is an understanding of the normal hospital postpartum timeline, so that you can prepare yourself for what will happen to most new babies in the first hours to days.

The Hospital System

In the hospital, nurses are the main people who take care of babies. They'll do all the initial weighing, measuring, and monitoring. If you are in a traditional hospital setting, a pediatric specialist, either your pediatrician (or someone from your pediatrician's group) or a pediatrician who

provides coverage for the hospital, will also check on your
baby to make sure everything is OK.

The nurses are your main source of help with breastfeeding while you're there. Take advantage of their expertise and
time to make sure you feel as confident as possible with the
way your baby is latching during breastfeeding. Because your
nurse will be coming into your room to check on you and
your baby at regular intervals throughout your stay, you'll
have multiple opportunities to ask your nurse to verify baby's
positioning at your breast and to assist as you start off on
your breastfeeding journey.

It may feel as if the doctor is never around. In fact, the
nurses have 24-7 private line access to a pediatric expert.
They will call right away if they are concerned about your
baby's feeding or health.

Following are common things to expect when your baby is
in the hospital.

Vitamin K Injection

Vitamin K is a substance in the blood that helps the clotting
process (*coagulation*). Clots are little clumps of platelets that
help keep your body from bleeding when it is not supposed
to. For example, when you scrape your knee, your body forms
a clot. Some people's bodies don't have enough of vitamin K
and cannot form these important little clumps. It wouldn't be
that big of a deal if we were just talking about scraped knees,
but clots are important in preventing bleedings in the brain,
in the gut, and everywhere in the body. It's very difficult to
know at birth who has and does not have enough vitamin K,
so all babies are given this as an injection in the hospital.

Erythromycin Ointment

When babies come through the birth canal, they are exposed to bacteria in the vaginal canal. Some of these are helpful ones that populate your baby's skin and his gastrointestinal tract, but some could be harmful. Although you may be 100% confident in your sexually transmitted infection (STI) status and, if you had prenatal care, could have had STI testing in pregnancy, erythromycin ointment is given. This is an ointment that we put into babies' eyes to make sure that, in the very off chance an infection was missed, the infection does not spread to the baby's eyes and cause permanent damage.

Bilirubin Testing

Jaundice is the yellow color of skin that results from a product called *bilirubin* in the blood. Bilirubin has healthy antioxidant properties and is useful in small amounts to us, but when there is too much, it can cross what is called the *blood-brain barrier* and cause problems in the brain.

Jaundice can be caused by a variety of things, but in the early days, one of the main reasons a baby gets jaundice is because he is not feeding well enough.

Twenty-four hours after birth, all babies in the hospital have a bilirubin test. This helps doctors see whether they need to do anything to intervene if the level is really high. A specific intervention called *phototherapy* (light therapy) can be used if the level of bilirubin is too high, and your nurse and provider can work together to figure out the cause of the jaundice. Typically, babies requiring phototherapy in the hospital are placed into an incubator with special lights attached along with a light-therapy blanket. During the treatment, your baby will wear a protective covering over his eyes.

Hepatitis B Vaccine

Hepatitis B is a serious disease that can affect the liver and lead to permanent damage or cancer. Although many people think of hepatitis B virus as affecting only users of IV (intravenous) drugs or those with high-risk sexual behaviors, it is highly contagious for a baby when she comes through the birth canal as well. Newborns especially are considered susceptible to hepatitis B virus and are more likely to have severe consequences. Some have acquired hepatitis B virus without known significant contact, so it is best to protect all babies from this virus and the serious disease it can cause.

The younger you are, the more likely you are to contract hepatitis B virus if you are exposed to it and the more likely you are to have permanent, serious problems from it. In my practice, we recommend the hepatitis B vaccine before discharge from the hospital, and then your baby will receive boosters later on in infancy.

Newborn Screening

Newborn screening is a public health effort to catch treatable diseases early on in babies that could otherwise be devastating, such as cystic fibrosis, thyroid disease, and metabolic disorders (of which babies can die suddenly because they can't process sugars or proteins correctly). All 50 states have a newborn screening program.

Getting your baby tested involves a tiny heel prick. The blood is then sent to the state and the screening program contacts you and your baby's doctor right away if there is an issue. No news is good news for the newborn screening program. Generally, this test is done in the first few days after birth. If your baby is born at a birthing center or leaves the hospital early, a second test by 2 weeks of age may be recommended.

Hearing Screening

All babies have a hearing screening before they leave the hospital. Some babies have a little bit of fluid in their ears when they are first born and will "fail" the screening for that reason. The hospital will set up a repeat screening or will give you instructions on how to arrange the repeat screening before you leave the hospital. It's really important to follow up if there was any initial concern, because hearing deficits can impede language development significantly, and if we catch them early, we can intervene as soon as possible.

Cardiac Screening

Several rare issues with a new baby's heart can manifest in the first few hours, days, or weeks after birth. Most hospitals have instituted a screening protocol to catch most of these issues. It can't catch everything, but it can catch a lot. A tiny, painless sensor, called an *oxygen saturation monitor,* will be put onto your baby. This will read how much oxygen is in your baby's blood, giving experts a great indicator of how her heart is doing.

The Hospital Timeline

For a baby born via vaginal delivery, most moms stay in the hospital for 2 nights. For cesarean deliveries, the general rule is 3 to 4 nights (federal legislation allows 48 hours for vaginal delivery and 96 hours for cesarean delivery).

Imagine you are in my hospital. In my hospital, a doctor performs an initial baby checkup within the first 24 hours after a baby is born, usually the morning after the baby has been delivered. On that first visit, we'll review what happened during the delivery, talk with the nurses about any concerns they have, come into the hospital room to talk with you about any concerns you have, examine your baby (the nurses will have already done this, but we do our own look), and make a plan for the day.

The plan is not that complicated: it's generally rest, eat, get as much help as you can from your nurses, and focus on learning how to feed your baby. Your early breast milk, called *colostrum,* has a *ton* of amazing benefits for your baby, such as antibodies and antioxidants, but there are small amounts of it, so you will need to feed frequently. In a few days, when your baby needs more milk, your supply will have increased.

Unless there are problems, such as your baby needs extra attention for feeding problems or the doctor has concerns about infection, we'll come back to see your baby on the day she is ready to be discharged from the hospital. On that day, we'll go over how to feed your baby and signs of infection to look for.

It's also important to set up an appointment with your baby's pediatrician. This appointment date depends on how things are progressing with your baby. For second-time parents and for parents of babies for which everything seems to be hunky-dory, we'll generally see you 2 to 3 days later. If we are concerned, we'll see you the next day in clinic.

My number 1 tip?

Stay in the hospital for the full amount of time your insurance allows if possible. A lot of parents ask me whether they can leave at the 24-hour mark. If things are OK with baby, that is a possibility, but I encourage them not to. Besides the actual delivery, the *second* 24 hours after birth are when babies tend to have issues.

Michelle and her partner could hardly wait to go home after their first little girl was born. They thought they would be more comfortable learning how to breastfeed in their own space instead of a hospital room. Besides, they lived only a few minutes from their pediatrician's office and

*it would be easy to take the baby in for visits as needed.
Michelle delivered her baby at 8:00 am on a Tuesday and
was home by noon on a Wednesday.*

*The first night after delivery, the baby was sleepy and
latched well. The second night, however, was more stressful.
Michelle and her partner struggled to help their baby latch
well and worried when she spit up a few times.*

*"We wished we stayed a little longer at the hospital," she
said to me in the office a few days later." Yes, our bed was
more comfortable and familiar, but **we** were not comfortable or familiar with taking care of our new baby yet, so
it didn't really matter. In the end, we could have used the
extra support and attention we received from the hospital's
nursing staff for a little longer."*

The Day You Go Home

When parents leave the hospital, I find that there is a range
of worrying, sometimes a little, sometimes a lot. It's a
Goldilocks situation that is very hard to understand. Even
the experienced freak out a bit. I freaked out with my first
child, and I had been giving parents advice for years about
how to raise a new baby. That's typical. You have fluctuating
hormones and you have never been responsible for another
human being before.

One important rule about newborns that many new parents soon learn: *they change rapidly,* and their needs are not
always consistent nor intuitive. What is true for their fluid
needs right at birth is extremely different from their needs
at 2 days, 3 days, and 4 days. Things ramp up really quickly
(or at least should), and things that seem like no big deal (a
small fever) can be a *really* big deal.

In all honesty, there really is no worrying too much when it comes to a newborn. What can happen, though, is the balance tips and you don't get the sleep you need because of anxiety, and your baby starts to pick up on the fact that you are uncomfortable.

The way to prevent this? Set yourself up with help from a lactation specialist or a doula so that you have a touch point along the way to reassure yourself and to guide you on the many little things that can go wrong. Ask for the doctor's appointment to be sooner once you are discharged. Stop searching the internet. Instead, look at or access reputable sources of information: doctors, nurses, lactation specialists, or quality books about newborns.

At our office, we also have a 24-hour nurse line. I encourage new parents to call this as often as they need to. "You are not bothering us when you call us," I say to parents. "You are the people we hope will call us when you are concerned."

The day you go home with your baby can be really awesome and a little terrifying. If you find yourself terrified, take a deep breath and consult the resources you have around you. I advise new parents to make a short emergency contact list for their phones or refrigerators before they head out the door and back into the "real world." Include the hospital, pediatrician advice line, close friends, and family.

CHAPTER 7

What's Typical, What's Not

When I was in medical school, we had a lengthy class on abnormal dermatologic findings, spread out over the course of months and integrated across various body system courses. When we learned about cancerous diseases, we also learned about the ways those problems manifest themselves in the skin.

In the beginning, someone in the class would inevitably start to panic that he had some horrible illness whenever we learned about a new condition, convinced he should call his family and arrange for a memorial service on the spot.

Over time, though, we became more accustomed to recognizing normal and abnormal findings in our patients and in ourselves (that is the point of medical training, it turns out). We transformed into confident, knowledgeable experts who used our rational observation and decision-making skills to come to diagnostic conclusions.

The same transformation happens for most new parents over time. At first, everything they notice on their newborns seems potentially serious. Each rash drives them to do a daylong Google search. Slowly, over time, they learn what they should worry about and what is to be expected.

A parent's education starts early in pregnancy with doctor visits and prenatal classes. The nursing staff at the hospital continues to inform and help new moms and dads and other parents, but things are so chaotic and new that it's really at the first doctor visit that what's typical and what's not tends to become more apparent.

Doctor Visits

Your newborn will have an appointment with your pediatrician a few days after leaving the hospital (give or take, depending on your situation) and again at 2 weeks of age. Between those 2 appointments, visits in the first 2 weeks are determined by need. Here are the issues that tend to bring babies back in sooner (your baby's doctor will let you know if your baby will need to be seen before then).

Newborn Weight Loss

Before a mom's milk supply increases, sometimes described as the milk "coming in," about 2 to 3 days after giving birth, a baby naturally loses a bit of weight. If your milk doesn't seem to be increasing, if your milk is ample but your baby is still not gaining weight, or if your baby continues losing weight beyond what is considered typical, we want to help your baby get on the right track.

This is super important in the first week: if a new baby doesn't get enough calories, her "blood sugar" (*blood glucose*) level can drop, which can make her sleepier and not want to eat as much. Sometimes she gets dehydrated, which makes everything worse. She doesn't have a lot of reserves, so she can start to spiral downward quickly. On the other hand, if we can get her moving in the right direction, she can bounce back with the energy she needs to thrive.

Jaundice

That first week is prime time for a baby to get jaundice.
While almost every baby has a tiny bit of jaundice, which
we call *physiological jaundice,* some babies reach a more
dangerous jaundice zone and need additional help (or at
least monitoring). Very rarely, this means going back to the
hospital, but often it means working on becoming more
hydrated and sometimes it means doing a home jaundice
treatment called a *bilirubin blanket.*

Feeding Issues

I've brought families back into my office for issues with
latching, for excessive spit-up, or *just because a parent is
concerned.* It's worth it to express your needs to me, because
I want you to get super comfy in your own skin as you start
to parent.

Signs of Illness

When you and your newborn go to the doctor for the first
time, we'll look closely for signs of infection and educate you
about what to look for so that you can spot illness right away.
You should call your newborn's doctor about these concerns
as soon as possible. (Remember, you are not a nuisance to
your pediatrician. You should feel comfortable calling and
asking your newborn's doctor questions. That is what doctors are there for.) If you are worried, call anyway. Figuring
out what you need to be worried about and what you don't
need to be worried about is part of the learning process as
you become parent. Better to be safe than sorry.

Persistent Fast Breathing

It's not typical for a baby to breathe fast consistently
(>1 breath per second) or to have what is commonly called
labored breathing for a sustained amount of time. I often

describe labored breathing to parents as sucking in at the ribs or the belly, flaring at the nose, or breathing hard as if the baby just ran a marathon. If your baby has persistent fast breathing, call your pediatrician's office right away. If she has sustained fast and labored breathing, call 911.

Fever 100.4°F (or 38°C) or Higher

You do not need to check your baby for a fever all day, every day. But if your baby seems fussy and is warm, check his temperature. When a newborn has a fever in the first month, it can signal a very serious infection in the blood, in the urine, or in the fluid surrounding the brain and spinal cord. Call your newborn's doctor's office for help with this, day or night.

Lethargy

Lethargy is a tough word because it means different things to different people. It doesn't just mean sleepy to medical professionals. To me, it means a baby is acting out of it enough that you could poke him with a stick and he wouldn't care. If a newborn misses more than one feeding, that could be a sign of lethargy. Lethargy is dangerous for babies. If you think your baby is lethargic, call your pediatrician's office immediately. If your baby is not responsive at all, call 911.

Projectile Vomiting

As indicated in the name, this is when vomit projects itself across the room. Spit-up that dribbles down the chin is not projectile vomiting. Projectile vomiting can be a sign of something called *pyloric stenosis,* when the connection between the stomach and the duodenum (the upper part of the small intestine) becomes too tight. Your pediatrician will want you to call immediately if your child has more than one episode of this.

Blood in Stool or Vomit

It's not typical to see blood in a newborn's vomit or stool (or persistent bleeding from anywhere, for that matter); this can signal a major issue in the digestive tract. Occasionally, if a mom's nipple cracks from breastfeeding trauma, a baby can swallow a little bit of blood and make us think it's the mom's blood, but don't take any chances. If you see blood, call your pediatrician.

Cyanosis

Cyanosis is a gray or blue color of the lips, of the inside the mouth, or on the chest. In a newborn, it can be very danger-ous, signaling infection or heart disease, especially if it comes on with feeding. Your pediatrician will want to know about this right away. If your baby has cyanosis and is not breath-ing, call 911. On the other hand, acrocyanosis, a purple, gray, or blue discoloration of the hands and feet, can be a typical newborn finding we attribute to an immature circulatory system.

Sweating or Panting During Feedings

If a baby pants or sweats while feeding, we worry that his body is stressed and that eating pushes it over the edge, taxing its basic metabolic functions. This can also be a sign of a dangerous infection or of heart disease. Call your baby's doctor right away if you notice this.

Severe Fussiness

Most babies are fussy, with a peak around 6 to 8 weeks after birth, but we worry when babies are completely inconsolable for hours on end. If your baby is fussy, first try changing her diaper, feeding her, burping her, and soothing her by swad-dling, swaying, or shushing her. If she's still crying after you've attended to all the baby care basics and exhausted all your soothing tricks, that warrants a call or a trip to the doctor.

Typical "Freak Out" Findings

On the other hand, these are a bunch of common findings that tend to really freak parents out, even though they are typical.

Erythema Toxicum

This is a completely benign rash with a scary name and a worrisome appearance: scattered red dots or splotches with white to yellowish centers. It tends to resolve on its own by 1 week after birth. You don't need to make a doctor visit for this rash, but it's reasonable to have it double-checked if you're worried or unsure, given new parents can occasionally confuse it with more troublesome viral or bacterial rashes.

Cross-eyed Appearance

A baby's eye muscles are often not strong enough to keep her eyes aligned until a few months of age. It can be typical for a baby's eyes to cross until about 3 to 4 months of age. If it lasts longer than expected, definitely let your pediatrician know.

No Poop for Days

When a baby is just out of the womb brand-new, pooping a lot means he is getting plenty of food. But after a few weeks, breastfed newborns can go up to 7 days without passing a stool (as long as it's mushy when it eventually comes out). As long as you're feeding your baby consistently, don't feel pressured to intervene to speed up the process. If your baby is gassy in the meantime, you can bicycle his legs and gently massage his belly. Once you get past the 7-day mark, let your pediatrician know. Also, let your pediatrician know if your baby has hard stools at any time. Your pediatrician will want to make sure feeding is going well and that your baby is growing as expected.

Hiccups

Just like the rest of a baby's nervous system is extremely immature, so is the diaphragm. Some babies hiccup a *ton* in the first few weeks. Don't sweat it. This is something that takes time to resolve on its own.

Congestion and Sneezing

Babies have been living in a water-filled environment for months when they're born—it's typical that they would need to clear out some of that fluid from the nasal passages. Babies have small nasal passages, so sneezing helps keep them open. If babies have even more fluid after several weeks, though, that's something to check with a doctor about. If they are coughing or sputtering during feedings, it may mean you need help with positioning or with overactive letdown.

Periodic Breathing

It's OK if a newborn's breathing is not completely uniform. Babies will often have episodes when they breathe fast for a few seconds and then go back to their usual rhythm. This should be brief, as opposed to the continuous fast breathing that makes pediatricians worry. If a baby has continuous fast or labored breathing, remember to seek immediate medical care.

The "Mini Period"

Baby girls may have a small amount of blood, or blood-tinged mucus, in the diaper at day 4 to 5 as their mothers' hormone (estrogen) levels begin to drop. This is like a "mini period," which can scare even the most confident parent. It may last for a few diapers before resolving. Large amounts of blood, however, are not typical, so consult a doctor if you notice this occurring.

A Stinky Umbilical Cord

When the umbilical cord falls off a baby, it can be kind of stinky. That's because the skin is dead. It's OK if there is a slight odor, but if there is extreme redness, swelling, or pus around the navel, parents should call their pediatrician right away—those are signs of potential infection.

Primitive Reflexes

Until babies are about 3 months old, they have what we call *primitive reflexes* (also known as startle movements). The most commonly recognized is the Moro reflex, when a baby puts her arms out to the side and jerkily flutters them forward when she has the sensation of falling (eg, when being set onto her back).

Slate Gray Patches

These are small areas of pigmented skin that can show up on the back or the buttocks. Occasionally, they are mistaken for bruises or can concern parents that they are dangerous, but they are harmless. They are especially common on the skin of black babies and babies of Asian ancestry.

Dry Skin

When babies are first born, their skin can look dry and flaky a few days after birth. They have been in water for a long time—it takes a while for the skin to adjust. This is not dangerous. Just let it be, and it will resolve on its own. You can use gentle products such as Aquaphor Healing Ointment or CeraVe Healing Ointment if the skin gets super dry and cracked in the creases of the ankles or wrists.

Babies don't need baths in the first few weeks after birth. They don't get that dirty. Obviously, clean their bottoms when they poop and spot clean if they spit up onto themselves, but otherwise, letting a baby's skin acclimate in the first few weeks without a bath is better, especially for umbilical cord healing.

Once you start giving baths, my favorite products are gentle cleansers. I love fancy, great-smelling, natural products just like the next mom, but they can often cause irritation. More basic options can help reduce the chance of rashes and other problems down the road.

CHAPTER 8

Setting Yourself Up for Breastfeeding Success

You're in the hospital, a new mom, trying to get your feet wet with the new baby feeding process. Well-wishers, relatives, and hospital staff all have a ton of advice. And given the gravity of the situation—the sinking feeling that you are now responsible for another human being and that his safety depends solely on you— it's understandable that you would be a little overwhelmed.

Angela was a new mom who cared deeply about breast-feeding her son. When I met her in my clinic for a meet and greet appointment at the end of her pregnancy, she had already taken a prenatal breastfeeding class but felt nervous about putting all that confusing education into action when the big day came.

"The instructor had a lot to say," she told me, "But I don't know if I'll remember it all. At about the 3-hour mark, my mind started to wander. I looked over at my girlfriend and she looked similarly dazed. The weekend before, we com-pleted a childbirth class and the next weekend we had a

baby care class. It's all running together now. If you asked me to tell you the most important fact the breastfeeding instructor taught me, I'm not sure I could regurgitate it."

Angela is not alone. Breastfeeding for the first time can be a daunting task, and while there are some amazing resources our there for fledgling feeders, sometimes, beginning by understanding the basics can be the most helpful.

These are the most important breastfeeding principles to help you feel confident as you start out.

Breastfeeding Specifics

You already know that babies need to eat. But the specifics of what they need and when they need it can be a bit more complicated.

Believe it or not, the first few days after birth have a huge influence on your breastfeeding success. No pressure, right? There is a ton you cannot control, so the most important concept is to know the basics of what to do when it goes right and then more specifically what can go wrong so that you can get help when you need it.

Watch Breastfeeding Videos

Watch videos about breastfeeding before you have your baby. The Stanford Medicine Newborn Nursery website (www.med. stanford.edu/newborns) has a great series about breastfeeding basics. Watch how the moms position their babies, and learn about latching properly. It will give you a book-level knowledge of what to do.

Get Latch Advice

When you are in the hospital, ask for help latching your baby right away. If possible, choose a hospital with nurses who are lactation certified so that you get professional help as soon as possible. The "gold standard" is to get your baby latched to your breast within 1 hour after birth, setting both of you up for success. The best way to achieve this is to have your baby placed skin to skin with you immediately after birth. Ask your nurse at the hospital to verify if the baby is positioned correctly. Ask for a lactation consultation if you have any concerns at all (this is pretty much every new mom I meet, so don't feel as if you have to have major worries in this area to justify getting extra assistance).

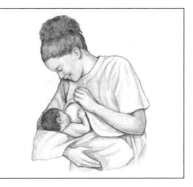

Feed Frequently

In the first few days to weeks, new babies need to have a feeding attempt at least every 3 hours. We call it "three hours start to start" in my office, which means it should be no longer than 3 hours from the start of one feeding to the start of another. Babies will often want to feed way more often than that, which is great and perfectly OK, but at the very least, they need that every-3-hour cueing.

Why? Breastfeeding is a 2-way feedback loop. The first feedback loop is for the mom: the more a baby's suckling stimulates the breast, the more milk the mom's body makes. The second feedback loop is for the baby: the more the baby eats, the more food he takes in and the more alert and hydrated the baby will be, driving hunger and allowing the baby to regulate his own feeding needs over time.

You may have heard 2 things that contradict this advice, so let me address them both.

First, people talk all the time about the fact that babies should feed on demand—that they should drive their own hunger and can do so, that breastfeeding should be natural. That's totally true...eventually. But in the beginning, a baby needs help getting her system going. Breastfeeding *is* natural, but it's not usually easy in the beginning for a new baby or a new mom—both have to learn new skills and how to rev up the system.

Second, there's a lot of talk in prenatal classes about how a baby's stomach is really small at first and how he doesn't need much milk, about how he really needs only the tiny bits of colostrum in the first few days. That is absolutely true. Babies are often sleepy in the first 24 hours after they are born, and mom's milk supply is limited in volume; the system is set up so that there's a little grace period.

But there's a catch: that is the time to prime the pump(s) by breastfeeding frequently so that the milk increases and so that baby is alert enough at day 3 to 4 to take the more copious milk mom starts making. In some cases, if that doesn't happen, "blood sugar" (*blood glucose*) levels can drop, making babies lethargic and harder to feed. Babies can get dehydrated, and their bilirubin levels can rise, contributing to jaundice (the yellow color that can develop in a baby's skin).

Learn Stimulation Techniques

Ask the nurses to teach you tricks to get your baby to continue being stimulated when on the breast, if she starts to fall asleep soon after the feeding begins. We use techniques such as "the chicken wing" (moving the baby's arm gently in a small circle), tickling her feet, using a cool cloth, and removing her clothing so that she is motivated to continue eating once she starts. Otherwise, the baby may burn energy on sucking without getting much back in return.

Understand Basic Biology

If you end up needing breastfeeding equipment such as nipple shields, make sure that you do extra pumping to offset the decreased stimulation to your breasts. Also, make sure that once your milk "comes in," you are what they call "fitted" for breast flanges (the cones that attach to the pump). Our lactation specialist says that if your breast flanges are not the right size, it's like walking around in shoes that are too big or too small.

Breastfeeding in the hospital can be hard because it's all so new. Once they go home, a lot of moms realize those hours clocked in the hospital were really the Golden Days—a time when they had tons of help and resources. Take full advantage of your time before you go home.

Breastfeeding Timeline

A basic understanding of the way breastfeeding usually progresses allows you to recognize when things aren't going quite as planned.

Breastfeeding Timeline			
What to Look For	**Days 1 to 2**	**Days 2 to 3**	**Days 4 to 5**
Breast milk	Colostrum thick, syrupy, yellow-gold, and nutrient dense	Milk "comes in" thinner, lighter yellow, and higher in volume.	Thin, skim milk appearance
Stool	1–2 wet Greenish black meconium stool	5–6 wet At least 3 dirty May look green or mix of dark brown and green	6+ wet At least 3 dirty May look yellow, seedy, and runny

What Can Go Wrong

Now, sometimes, health issues or difficulties can arise or not go as planned. Most people do not talk much about this. I think it is in the name of not making people panic, but the reality is that breastfeeding can be challenging. A lot of moms tell me they wish that someone had been real with them about that aspect.

Difficulty Latching

It can feel uncomfortable at first when most babies learn to breastfeed because their suction is stronger than anything their mothers' breasts have ever experienced. But if the pain is severe or persistent, you need to get help. Pain in the first days is often caused by a poor latch. If you have nurses or a lactation specialist help you in the hospital, having either help you assess latch is one of the most important things you can do. This is one of those things that is impossible to know until you are doing it—watching a video can help you know the basics of latching, but it can't replace the real thing.

Excessive Weight Loss

If your baby isn't getting enough milk, she can lose too much weight. By about day 3 to day 4, your milk should be in. You'll start to see and hear your baby really swallowing when she is eating, and you may see milk at the corner of her mouth. If that isn't happening, again, it means you need help.

We expect that babies will lose up to 10% of their birth weight in the first few days after birth. But once your milk is well established, weight gain begins.

One of the major indicators of a normal progression is poop, which changes rapidly as your milk comes in.

It is important to know that babies who are breastfed exclusively have very loose stools that are easy to pass. Some new parents mistake these typical stools for diarrhea.

Poop Changes in the First Week		
Day	Number	Color
1-2	1-2	Greenish black meconium
2-3	3+	Green or mix of dark green and brown
4-5	3+	Yellow, seedy, and runny

Difficulty Handling Feedings

All babies have a very floppy connection between the feeding tube (esophagus) and the stomach. This is called the *lower esophageal sphincter*. This acts as the gatekeeper for contents to pass through to the stomach. When this muscle is loose, it typically causes your baby to spit up. Pyloric stenosis typically causes babies to spit up around 1 month of age as well as can cause forceful and frequent vomiting, eventually leading to projectile vomiting. Consult your baby's doctor sooner rather than later if projectile vomiting progresses.

Sometimes, though, if your milk is coming out superfast (called *overactive letdown*) or if your baby is spitting up all day, every day, it may be uncomfortable for your baby to eat. A lactation specialist can help you assess this and give you tips for positioning and for decreasing the flow to your baby.

Finding Assistance

About 20% of women choose not to breastfeed at all, but for the other 80%, many stop breastfeeding earlier than they intended. Only 25% are still exclusively breastfeeding at 6 months.

There are huge differences between communities around the world with large and small rates of breastfeeding success. In successful communities, new breastfeeding moms have extreme support from experienced breastfeeders. They also expect that breastfeeding will take time and effort to establish. Sometimes a new parent doesn't realize the questions or issues she has until an expert helps.

The solution for many moms in modern America? Hands-on support from a lactation specialist. That way, as long as you recognize the challenges you may be encountering, you can make adjustments right away, not several days later. Things change quickly with babies. What is true for their health needs at day 3 can be very different at day 5. So if something is not working well at day 3, you want to address it quickly so that it isn't a major issue later.

The best way to receive the right lactation help is to know your lactation resources and have them set up before you have your baby. Also, realize that hospital-based lactation specialists may have a different perspective than someone who primarily cares for babies once they are out of the hospital. Our lactation specialists in clinic see a range of babies from birth to 12 months, even 24 months, so they feel really comfy moving moms through all the stages of lactation.

The following options are the best resources for finding lactation help.

In-home Lactation

If you can swing it financially, a board-certified lactation specialist who comes to your home multiple times in the first few weeks is best. These specialists can assess your individual needs in your home environment. They should also be able to help you get through snags, because they are working directly with you and seeing your home setup.

When searching for a specialist, make sure you look for a lactation specialist who has a current International Board-Certified Lactation Consultant status. That way, you'll find someone credible and reliable and who is as up-to-date as possible on current breastfeeding recommendations.

Clinic-Based Lactation

Call your potential pediatric office to see whether they have someone there who can help you. If they have someone who comes into each first visit, great. If not, ask for that once you arrive for your first baby appointment.

Hospital-Based Lactation

These experts are invaluable. They'll work with you right after delivery to help you feel confident in the first several days postpartum, but they'll also provide breastfeeding support to moms who have questions and need extra help after they leave the hospital. Hospital-based lactation specialists are especially important for moms who live in geographic areas without many other community lactation resources. If you're considering using a hospital-based lactation specialist after your hospital stay, ask the hospital staff for help setting up your appointment so that you have less to arrange when you're back home.

Doulas

Doulas can work well if they are board-certified in lactation as well as certified to help with your postpartum care. You're not just looking for opinions here; rather, you want someone who is confident and knows what is being talked about from a trained perspective.

Family Help

This really depends on you and your needs. For me, I found it difficult to have a family member hovering around me while I worked on learning how to breastfeed my daughter. Even though my family meant well, their breastfeeding skills were rusty, so I found that they were greatest support for things such as laundry and meal preparation. If you have other children, this is a great time for them to help keep them busy, fed, and put to bed at their regular time(s).

If breastfeeding just doesn't work for you, please remember, breastfeeding does *not* define you as a mom. It's one small part of your motherhood journey. Being a mom is about *so* much more than breastfeeding.

Finding lactation help is one of the most important parts of breastfeeding success. Thank goodness there are caring, professional lactation experts waiting to guide you through the ups and downs of breastfeeding your baby.

If you're using formula, remember these storage and preparation tips.

Pay Attention to Formula Preparation

If you are formula feeding, take advantage of your ability to prepare ahead and to carry food portably. You can make a batch of formula in advance for the day (refrigerated continuously for up to 24 hours). Consider using a formula mixing pitcher for mixing larger amounts. This cuts down on the air bubbles that get introduced with shaking a bottle. Premeasured packets can help you feed your baby safely and easily if you're on the go.

Be Safe When Storing Prepared Formula and When Heating Bottles

Once you prepare a bottle of formula, feed it to your baby or put it into the refrigerator within 1 hour. If it's been at room temperature for more than an hour, throw it out. If you make a bottle of formula for your baby and she doesn't drink the whole thing, discard it. You can prepare formula up to 24 hours ahead of time by storing it in the refrigerator (so that it doesn't form bacteria). If you open ready-made formula containers, they can be stored safely in the refrigerator for up to 48 hours.

Take Caution When Heating Bottles

Just because most people heat their babies' bottles, it's not necessary. A lot of babies will tolerate cold or room temperature bottles of formula just fine, saving you headaches and time in the long run. If your baby prefers a warm bottle, never use a microwave to heat it. The microwave can create "hot spots" within the formula, leading to potential burns. Instead, run the bottle under hot or warm water for a few minutes or use a pan of hot water to heat the liquid. Bottle warmers also work well. However you heat your baby's bottles, make sure to shake them well after heating and to test the formula temperature by placing a few drops onto the inside of your wrist to assure it's lukewarm (not hot).

CHAPTER 9

At Home in the First Few Weeks

By the end of next year, you will be a seasoned parent. You'll be a pro at a lot of things. Not in that "Oh, yeah, babies are hard" kind of way. More like "I understand that this stage takes around 2 days to pass. I believe it will pass because there was a time 3 days ago that the very same thing happened and it passed." Timelines and stages will be etched in your memory.

But if you haven't had a baby before, visualizing what's ahead and asking others about their experiences, plus reading credible information from reliable sources, can make those early days easier. Still, it is really useful to have at least some basic information about what is typical in the first few weeks so that, when you are caught off guard, you can refer back to it.

Keeping Baby Safe

The number 1 thing moms and dads and other parents learn when they become new parents? Not much is under your control. You can, though, take a few steps to set yourself up for as much success as possible.

Vaccinations are important

Making sure that you and the people who come in close contact with your baby have all their vaccinations is super important. Vaccine-preventable infections such as whooping cough (*pertussis*) and even the flu can cause serious symptoms in all people, especially babies, so I recommend all the vaccines on the Centers for Disease Control and Prevention vaccine schedule. (Please see the *2019 Recommended Immunizations for Children from Birth Through 6 Years Old* on pages 156 and 157. For the most current and updated schedule, please visit www.cdc.gov/vaccines/schedules/easy-to-read/child-shell-easyread.html.)

Avoid sick people

Now may not be the best time to take your baby to the company picnic or holiday party. Let your family members hold your new one, but first make sure they are not sick. A trip to a crowded store is not on my list of recommended activities. But if you want to go outside, take your baby on a short walk in the stroller with an appropriate weather canopy and an extra layer of warmth, if needed.

Pay attention to handwashing

Make sure that all who touch or hold your baby first thoroughly wash their hands, each time, with warm, soapy water. Don't be shy about asking your friends and family members to do this. They will all understand that you are trying to keep the germs away from your newborn.

Limit air travel

The first month after your baby is born is not the time to expose your baby to recycled air on an airplane or around a host of people you do not know (and germs) in the airport. How often have you gotten sick after traveling? I don't recommend air travel until babies have had their first set of vaccines, which can happen at 6 weeks at the earliest.

Prevent falls

Babies can be slippery little people. Make sure you have a hand on your baby at all times if she is on an elevated surface. I have, unfortunately, had parents call my office multiple times after their babies fell out of beds or off of changing tables. It scares me when I see a baby by herself on an examination table in the office. You never know when she is going to roll slightly or propel herself in one direction or another. It's always important to keep one hand on your baby at all times.

Reduce suffocation risk

When it comes to your baby's sleep, a lot of new products come and go in the mommy circles. Don't be fooled. Even if "everyone" is using the newest sleep gadget, it doesn't mean it's safe or approved for sleep. Don't use blankets or stuffed animals in the sleep area. Make sure swaddle blankets don't cover your baby's mouth. Back to sleep is best. Avoid side or stomach sleep positions.

Your Growing Baby

One of my favorite things to do is see new babies in the office. As your baby grows, your pediatrician will offer what we call *anticipatory guidance,* not just to prevent injury and illness but also to help your baby reach his full potential when it comes to development, growth, and wellness.

At each doctor's appointment, we weigh your baby, perform a physical examination, and talk with you about what is going well, what you need help with, and what you can expect until the next visit. We also take a look at vaccination status and make sure your baby received the newborn screening in the hospital, that the hearing screening was passed, and that there were no heart concerns while your baby was there.

Remember, your baby's doctor is there to help you and guide you as you navigate those challenging early days.

The Tough Moments

The first 2 weeks are all about—you guessed it—learning the feeding patterns and habits. New babies tend to do a lot of cluster feeding during these weeks, when they just finish feeding and then seem to want to feed again 20 minutes later. They also sleep sporadically and are just getting used to their environment outside the womb. Here are the top 4 things parents consistently tell me are tough about those first 2 weeks and what you can do to address them.

Avoid diaper rashes

Diaper rashes are very common because your baby's outer layer of skin is significantly thinner than an adult's, making it more vulnerable to damage. The diaper area is dark, warm, and wet—the perfect place for yeasts and bacteria to breed. Your baby is pooping and peeing all day long. Plus, the materials in most baby wipes can be super irritating, even if they are labeled as natural.

WHAT CAN YOU DO ABOUT IT?

- Change diapers right away. If your baby is sleeping and has a wet diaper, don't feel as if you need to wake her up to change it. But otherwise, change her diaper so that those irritants are off your baby's skin.

- Use diaper creams with a barrier component as soon as possible at the first sign of a rash, and use them with *each* diaper change until the rash goes away. Apply diaper creams like cupcake frosting—you want a thick barrier so that the next time your baby urinates, the skin doesn't get even more irritated, preventing the skin from healing.

- Choose good wipes. Those indicated for sensitive skin or that are water based tend to work well. A lot of parents get very excited about fancy wipes. Unfortunately, even wipes that are labeled as "organic" or "natural" can have products in them that irritate a baby's bottom. This is an area in which basic is better.

- Consult your baby's doctor if the rash doesn't start to go away after a few days or it looks different from just redness or irritation. Doctors can help you figure out if you need a prescription medication to help cure the yeast or bacterium.

Expect spit-up

It's typical for all babies to spit up, and most of the time, it is just a laundry issue. Every once in a while, though, it can cause discomfort for babies and can make successful breastfeeding difficult.

WHAT CAN YOU DO ABOUT IT?

- Position your baby's head higher than her body during feedings, and hold her body upright after feedings. This allows the food to go down instead of up. Think about yourself when you eat a huge meal. You feel uncomfortable, right? You feel like burping. You might even feel a little bit of spit-up coming up. If you were to lie down, you would feel even worse. The same goes for a baby.

- Burp your baby often during feedings. This allows the air bubbles to come up and the food to go down. If you are using a bottle, use a slower-flow nipple. This creates less of a firehose scenario for your baby when she is trying to feed.

- If you are breastfeeding, ask your baby's doctor or lactation specialist about laid-back positioning and about C clamping if it seems as if you may have overactive letdown. Signs include your baby having a hard time handling the amount of milk that comes into his mouth, milk spraying everywhere when your breasts let down, or you having so much milk at your initial letdown that you have to catch a bunch of it in a towel or it gets all over you and your baby.

- Laid-back breastfeeding positioning is just that—you recline back onto a pillow or a couch so that you're at more of a 45° angle with your baby, as opposed to leaning over your baby's mouth, so that the milk flows more like a stream instead of a waterfall (which is less forceful).

- C clamping is when you make a C shape with your forefinger and your thumb, encircling your breast just behind the areola. You latch your baby, watch your baby swallow your first letdown's milk, and then, instead of clamping down and pushing forward, you clamp down and push back onto the breast tissue to stop the flow. Wait until your baby takes a pause from eating, then loosen your clamp. Repeat this for the rest of the feeding until your baby is done eating. Again, your pediatrician or lactation consultant will be the best person to let you know if this is appropriate for you.

Fight against superhuman levels of fatigue

When you are a new parent, sleep deprivation is your biggest enemy. If you can get the sleep you need, everything is much better.

You're all hyped up on hormones and anxiety. In the very beginning, the adrenaline coursing through your body really messes with your sleep. In the beginning, you will notice every little sound your baby makes, making it really difficult to get the shut-eye you need. By the time all that dies down, you're left exhausted and feeling behind the eight ball.

Plus, you tend to have a lot of family around, and that can tire you out, as you are always feeling like a host. At my core, I am an introvert, and that personality trait did not change the second I had a baby. If you are an introvert too, the same will be true for you. In fact, your natural tendency will probably get stronger.

You'll need a specific plan given that the postpartum period tends to be a particularly social one. When you have a new little one, people want to make you dinner and help you out as much as possible. They want to see the new baby and hold the new baby. Family, especially, wants to spend precious time with you right away. They also want to socialize with you. They are excited about your bundle of joy and want to talk all about it.

Add in that your baby snoozes all day and is awake all night and—*boom!*—the perfect recipe for disaster.

Sometimes the daytime sleeping tricks you into feeling as if you could get a bunch of chores done during the day. Your energy is up, and you feel as if you might as well get out of the house or at least put in a load of laundry. But then nighttime comes and everything goes haywire. Unless your houseguests are there to be on night duty, it's just you (and your partner, I hope) up all night trying to figure things out and soothe your new baby and not disturb your houseguests.

WHAT CAN YOU DO ABOUT IT?

- Have times in the first few weeks *every day* when you are completely off duty except to feed. Put in ear plugs, go to a separate area of the house, and have your partner come get you up when baby needs to eat, but otherwise, be free in your own home, even if it is for 5 minutes.

- Before the nighttime activity gets going, rest. It sounds lame, but going to bed at about 7:00 pm, after you do your last evening feeding, allows you get in a solid 1 or 2 (maybe 3) hours before the night shift starts. Have the baby in a room with another awake caregiver while you sleep solo for a few hours before nighttime really hits. The point is to get some solid shut-eye without interruption. Then, when you get woken up again a few hours later for your baby's next feeding, you know you at least have those few hours under your belt. Then, you can move your baby to your room when he's ready, finally, to sleep as nighttime officially starts.

- I did not do that with my first daughter, but with my second, I made it a point to, and it was a *game changer.* It really took the fear out of the nighttime sleep situation.

Expect boredom with your baby

When babies are first born, they don't do much. They sleep and eat and then sleep some more. When they are awake, it can be difficult to know how or if to stimulate them. Should you buy a bunch of developmental toys? Does your baby need fancy activity mats or baby flash cards? Not necessarily.

WHAT CAN YOU DO ABOUT IT?

- Instead of focusing on commercial products, go back to basics. Read, read, read. It doesn't have to be baby books in the first few weeks to month. Read your own novels out loud. Reading and talking to our babies enhances communication, reducing frustrations as they learn to ask for what they want and need but also fostering social connections and building parent-baby bonds. Research shows that the more words parents use when speaking to an 8-month-old infant (it can be a difference of 30 million words from one family to another!), the greater the size the child's vocabulary will be at age 3.

- I love having background music on in the house. Both my babies "went" to multiple concerts when they were in my belly, and they'd been out dancing and swaying before they came into the world. The best thing for them, though, is when they actually hear the people they love singing to them, looking into their eyes, or dancing around with them.

Nighttime Sleep

Arm yourself with 4 bits of knowledge

They were straight-up petrified. A mom- and dad-to-be, sitting there on the couch in my pediatrics office. Wide-eyed and hopeful, hopped-up on information about "this year's best stroller." Filled to the brim with platitudes their friends and family all offered about what to expect when the timer dinged on their little bun in the oven. "It'll be hard, but you'll love it. Enjoy your sleep now, 'cause it will never be the same again."

They had heard it all for months, and now they were looking for real answers as to what would happen to their lives in those first few weeks. Real answers to the steps they could actually take to prepare themselves for the new little baby who was about to enter their world and turn it completely upside down.

I see it all the time in prenatal meet and greet appointments in my clinic—the fear, the trepidation, to bring up the main question that is on (pretty much) everyone's mind: How do I get my baby to sleep? Good news is, I've got the answer. Before we get to the strategy part, these 4 bits of knowledge are key.

BABIES DON'T GET IT

Babies don't realize we're living in the modern world. They have no idea that you have a limited maternity leave. It doesn't matter to them that you've already lived 35 years and have a social life. They certainly don't care if you have a certain level of sleep you're used to. Their needs and desires are the same as the needs babies had thousands of years ago.

When they are first born (and for the first 3 months afterward), they want only to keep things going as they were in that blissful, dark, loud, warm, cozy womb from which they just came.

BABIES ARE MIXED-UP

Newborns have their days and nights completely switched up. Before birth, your baby is swayed by the motion of your body throughout the day, lulled to sleep by the small and large movements you make. At night, it's party time. If you are pregnant and reading this right now, you know *exactly* what I mean. It's reassuring on some level to feel a baby kicking around all night long, but it's also hard to get any shut-eye some nights. All throughout the night, your body is not in motion, so your baby thinks it's time to get active. Once you deliver your newborn, it takes a while for him to catch the drift that night is actually night and day is actually day.

YOU GET IT

You realize you live in the modern world. I know, I know, you already know that. That's why you're probably scared about this in the first place, right? But a new parent's perspective gets thwarted easily. Somewhere along the line, people tend to forget a basic premise: this is not like all the modern things you typically do. They start trying to fix things instead. They try to make their baby get onto a sleep schedule starting week 1 (I think that bedtime routines and sleep schedules can be a great thing; they're just not the solution really early on for most babies). They buy every product known. They fight and fight to get their baby to sleep.

I've been there too. I've gotten frustrated with my baby, with my husband, and with the whole lack of sleep situation. Even though I was already an expert in baby health and care when my first child was born, I lost sight sometimes in the early days that sometimes you can't fix it. You just have to let it ride out, for a little while. The times I was able to accept that truth in my early parenthood experience were my most successful.

Let me give you a nonbaby example: think of the last really challenging exercise class or workout you did. The one when you had to psych yourself up even to make it down to the studio or to strap on those running shoes, because you just *knew* that there would be a moment when you'd think, "This is so hard." Think of the moment you had to tell yourself, "Just keep breathing; use your resources (distracting yourself with music, focusing on your form, or thinking about your goal)." Think about how, at some point, your options were to give up or to keep pushing through.

There wasn't anything you could do to make it substantially better; you just had to keep going. That's kind of how, on some level, you have to approach new baby sleep. In the beginning, there are only so many things you can control (we'll get to these in a second). Instead, you have to focus more on your own resources so that *you* can get through the tough time with resilience.

BABIES DON'T ALWAYS FOLLOW THE BOOK

Your baby may not do what the baby sleep books tell him to do. If someone tells you that she can get *every* baby to sleep well *every night* using her methods, you've gotta be a little wary. I mean, come on, you are smart enough never to buy that when it comes to anything else in your life (think get rich quick schemes and perfect beauty tricks), so why would it be true for baby sleep, when families and babies are all so individual? No, babies are like Frank Sinatra—they do it *their way.*

A child's temperament is a huge influencer of how well he sleeps from the very, very beginning. Environment and parents sure help, but in the end, temperament always plays a huge role. Some babies are just better sleepers than others. My first baby was all kinds of colicky. She just did *not* sleep at night. I worked and worked and worked at it, and eventually, she got it down, but it was definitely a full-time job for a while. My second daughter, on the other hand, followed the baby sleep handbook. She fell asleep easily, woke happily, and then did it all again a few hours later.

I'm not telling you this to scare you. I'm telling you because if you have a baby who doesn't like to sleep or has a hard time getting into the rhythm, you shouldn't beat yourself up about it. It is not your fault. It's just the way your sweet baby is wired. One day, your baby will probably be CEO of a Fortune 500 company. But for those first 5 to 6 months of life, it might be a little rough in the sleep department. Repeat after me: "I *will* get through this."

Feeling defeated? Don't. There is a way to get through the throes of newborn sleeplessness with grace and resilience.

Get through with grace and resilience

SET YOURSELF UP FOR SUCCESS

Create an environment that is conducive to good sleep at night. Make the room dark; get the white noise going. Watch online videos of how to soothe your baby.

Don't expect that it will work perfectly. You want to avoid feeling stuck, as if you have no tricks up your sleeve. Get the basics down ahead of time and add to your toolbox as you go, making lists of calming tricks if you need to and putting them onto your fridge or phone so that you can refer to them as you get familiar with what works for your baby.

The American Academy of Pediatrics recommends that babies be put to bed by themselves onto their backs on a flat surface with a tightly fitted sheet and no extra bedding or pillows to prevent sudden infant death syndrome. I wholeheartedly agree with this recommendation.

If you use something other than a swaddle blanket to wrap your baby, you'll likely look on a site such as Amazon or Target for advice on what to purchase. Like most other gear for babies, if an item gets ten thousand 5-star customer reviews, it's a great place to start, but it still might not be the best for *your* baby. You might have to try things out to see what will work for you and your family. Remember to check out safety information on sites such as Consumer Reports (www.consumerreports.org)—just because something is available online does not mean that it is a safe product for a baby. When swaddling, make sure that the baby's hips and legs are slightly flexed, instead of fully straightened, and that the legs are not too tightly wrapped. This prevents problems with the development of the hips. Sleep sacks can keep the hips in a better position.

ADDRESS YOUR OWN SLEEP NEEDS

This is the most important tip I can give parents about their newborn and sleep. When I finished residency, I thought I would be all set to deal with sleep deprivation. I was used to staying up all night long, sometimes for up to 30 hours at a time for one shift. But the thing I forgot when I got into the whole new baby thing was that I was also accustomed, at some point, to having uninterrupted rest for hours at a time. Plus some weekends off. That is very different from the sinking feeling that you may never sleep again when your baby is brand-new. While you can't completely control how your baby sleeps, you can make sure you optimize your own sleep. Here's how.

You need to feed your baby really frequently in the early days and weeks, but you don't need to be the only one who soothes her in between feeding sessions. That means your partner (or someone else—a family member or a postpartum doula) needs to step in and become soother in chief for a while. Otherwise, you will be at higher risk for postpartum depression and anxiety, and possibly resent the people around you, and be less able to enjoy your baby during the day. If (again, back to our ancestors) you lived with all 20 of your favorite relatives in one common dwelling, this would be easy. In our culture of isolation, it can be tricky for some new moms to find help, but it is so very worth it.

Even if you have someone designated as a soother in chief every other night for 1 week, it will do wonders for your mental and physical health. The whole point is having a time in the future you can look forward to when you know you will get sleep (even if that time is 2 days away).

PUT YOUR BABY TO SLEEP AWAKE

While your baby is still in the snoozy phase, try to put your baby to sleep while he is still slightly awake so that he gets used to falling asleep on his own.

SAFE SLEEP ENVIRONMENT

The American Academy of Pediatrics recommends that babies sleep in their parents' room for at least the first 6 months after birth but not in their parents' bed. Evidence has shown that room sharing is associated with a reduced risk of sudden infant death. No one who is high or drunk should sleep in the same bed with a child. Ideally, pets and other children should not be sleeping in the bed either. Remove all blankets, pillows, and bumper pads from your baby's crib. Babies should be placed onto their back on a firm sleep surface, such as a firm crib mattress with a fitted sheet. Don't sleep in recliners or couches with your baby. The risk of unintentional suffocation is higher than in a bed.

WAIT IT OUT

Be patient with your baby and with yourself. For some babies, sleep is great right away, but for others, you've got to wade through the murky water until you get to the fresh stream a little farther ahead. Use your resources and mind-fulness, just like you would for any other challenging obstacle in your life. Of course, if your baby seems excessively fussy or you are concerned about illness, seek help from your baby's pediatrician. Get help from a lactation consultant if things seem to be haywire in the feeding department.

Lana and Peter were parents who had to wait it out. Lana read every book under the sun and hired in-home doulas to help her during the night, but her baby still did not sleep well. She listened to her friends talk about their angelic babies and wished she had the same experience they did, but, in the end, there was nothing she could do but give it time.

Now that Lana's baby is 2 years old, those sleepless nights are a distant memory, but in the moment, they seemed to go on forever.

"I remember the first time my daughter slept more than 4 hours at a time," she told me. "I remember realizing there was nothing I did to make it finally happen. One day it just did."

So is it possible for a newborn to "sleep like a baby"? Well, technically, yes. Newborns will sleep like the immature, womb-seeking, still developing humans they are. That's the truth. Remember how primitive your baby's needs are. Get your mind right. Get educated about how to soothe a baby and set up a sleep environment that optimizes rest for both of you. Above all, because babies aren't modernizing anytime soon, make sure you get *your* sleep by forming a solid team around you from the get-go. That way, even if your baby isn't quite up to speed on how to calm and sleep when he first arrives, you can teach him with patience and perspective until he finds his way.

Daytime Sleep and Carrying

During the day, baby swings can be super helpful if you are observing your baby in them and your baby is awake. Just remember that your goal is to get your baby to engage in less rocking and swaying during the day once you get your rhythm with feeding, so some times without those products are great. Also, they are not designed for sleep.

Carrying your baby has also been proven to reduce colic and, obviously, to help you bond with your baby.

There are a lot of options out there for carriers. I'm going to be honest and say that the long-piece-of-fabric varieties just never worked for me. I watched many tutorial videos on how to put them on, but my babies always "hated" them. The good news? This is an area in which the sky's the limit, and the baby blogs are full of reviews.

Soothing

He was holding her as if she might bite him, his arms outstretched and awkward, shoulders tense. The baby was crying, her arms also outstretched and flailing, as he tried to half bounce, half shush her. It was almost painful to watch.

"She doesn't like me. She only wants her mom," he told me at our first health supervision checkup in the office. "I've never been around babies. I don't have any clue what to do with them."

His face looked lost, surprised, and defeated. He felt as if he could not contribute and wondered if he would ever bond with the little alien being who had just arrived via his wife's body. (I know this sounds strange, but the things that go through your mind as a new parent often are.)

My husband said he felt the same way when he held my daughter for the first time. Many new parents tell me they feel this way; unfortunately, it can be a self-perpetuating cycle of defeat when you feel as if each time it's your turn to soothe your baby, your baby somehow gets crankier and crankier.

You know how they say bees can smell fear? It's clear that newborns can too. Well, maybe not smell it, but at least they can sense it. If you're not relaxed as you try to relax them, they know it.

We spent 15 minutes that day walking through the basics of soothing a baby. In the end, he was by no means the baby whisperer, but he had the information and tools he needed to keep trying to bond with his little one.

Soothing your baby falls into 2 categories: getting ahold of yourself and then attending to your baby's needs. You've heard the phrase on an airplane "Put the mask on yourself first"? That applies here as well. Earlier, we talked about getting your mind-set right when it comes to having a baby. Here we'll talk about soothing your little one.

Our goal as parents should be to mimic the intrauterine environment from which they just came, which is dark, very loud (think blood rushing around and a loud heartbeat), almost constantly in motion (except when you are sleeping—that's why babies tend to be more active in the evenings), and quite compact and secure.

When You're Not the Mom You'd Hoped You'd Be

She was already crying when I opened the door to the examination room. She sat defeated, her newborn snuggled closely in her arms, huge tears rolling down her cheeks. Try as she might, she could not get the latch right when she tried to breastfed. She told me she must be one of those "breastfeeding failures." She had spent the past 4 days in pain as her baby clamped down onto her again and again. Now, exhausted and defeated, she wasn't sure how to move forward.

I watched as she told me her story, her shoulders heaving as she took gulping breaths between sobs. I knew what she really meant: "I feel like I have already failed at this whole mother thing and I am less than a week into it. I am not the parent I'd hoped I would be."

Don't let disappointment define you

Breastfeeding is a parenting area ripe for disappointment. Society puts a ton of pressure on moms-to-be and then doesn't educate them well before their babies are born on the potential pitfalls of this not-so-intuitive task. After birth, support from other experienced breastfeeders is usually minimal at home. Add in that we often put the onus on moms to do most of the day and night care within a family and—*bam!*—Stress City, here we come.

Of course, as a pediatrician, I support the Breast Is Best movement when possible. The benefits of breast milk and breastfeeding are super clear, and I want to help breastfeeding parents reach their breastfeeding goals. But those who cannot or do not breastfeed often feel (or are made to feel) as if they are somehow parenting failures because of their struggles or decisions in this *one area.*

Breastfeeding is not the only opportunity to feel, potentially, like a parenting failure. What about when we raise our voice at our toddler when we're stressed or realize we've been ignoring our baby while we peruse our social media feed? How about the time my doctor friend missed her own kid's case of pneumonia? Yeah, those feel like real Mother of the Year moments too.

Understand your real fears

What about the bigger, longer-term fears new parents have? That the core issues we deal with ourselves are going to royally ruin our kids in some way? Your mild anxiety (or your a-little-too-laid-back personality), your own parents' failures, your lack of expertise in all things child related— all these insecurities can get in the way of doing your best day by day.

One mom in my office put it so well: "I handle multi-million-dollar sales transactions daily. I sit in a conference room with other business leaders and can influence their decision-making at the drop of a hat. But getting my toddler to put on her shirt? Somehow, I fail every day at doing that without getting flustered and losing my cool. It's so demoralizing. I'm scared of what I'll mess up when she gets older and it really counts."

Social media feeds our worries on this as well. You've seen the articles: "10 Things That Will Mess Up Your Relationship With Your Teenager," "The 5 Tips You Need to Raise Brave Girls." They are well-intentioned, and they often have really useful information, but read enough of them and, in the end, they can leave you feeling stuck, not motivated, if consumed without the right perspective.

Our friends, our parents, and our significant others— pressure and guilt can come from all sides, piling on a sense that it's all-or-nothing. That good enough is never enough. That only the best will do.

The real secret to successful parenting is understanding and dealing with our own personal struggles and pain points, not pretending they don't exist or acting as if we just smile a little brighter, others won't notice our humanity. Going to therapy, or to lactation, or to the pediatrician for help. Understanding we are not as in control as we think we are most of the time. That sometimes we do our best and take all the classes and read all the books and *it still doesn't work.*

Taking a look at our own "weaknesses" and fears—these are the things that really make a difference.

I looked that sobbing mom in the eye, took her hands, and told her what countless moms (including me) have needed to hear at some time or another: "You are an amazing mother. What or how you feed your baby does not define that. In fact, you can use that you overcame this challenge (either breastfeeding in the end *or not*) to show your baby how to be resilient in his own life. All moms have moments when they realize it is impossible to be flawless and that it is better, in the end, not to be. You are more than OK. You are just what your baby needs."

Of course, that's when I started tearing up right alongside her.

I knew some reassurance would help, but the look of relief that washed over that new mom's face? It was stunning to see her whole body relax and her demeanor change.

Baby and mom ended up just fine. They found their way. We got mom the help she needed, but more important, we addressed one of the most foundational worries of motherhood directly.

~: *The Day Your Baby Arrives* :~

I want to tell you that you are going to be an amazing mom. Don't worry about being a perfect mom. Remember that on your best days and on your worst days. Remind yourself that your baby is a gift specifically meant for you. Don't beat yourself up if just a few days or weeks into this thing called *motherhood,* you do not feel as if you are the parent you'd hoped you would be. None of us are. But you have the resources here to start you on your way.

Years from now, whether you're tending to your 3-year-old's scraped knee or patching up your teenager's bruised ego, you'll still see him as your little baby, and you'll still remember the monumental moment you became his mom. You'll remember holding him for the first time and telling him you're going to try to be the best mom ever but that you'll need a little grace along the way to do it.

Try your very best. Lean on your partner. Take time to reset when you need it. Deal with your own issues head-on; get the help you need to support yourself and provide yourself with the parenting tools that will allow you to rise above your most challenging days. Know your baby will learn the most about how to grow into a healthy adult as he watches you authentically work to take care of him to the best of your ability while, at the same time, making space to take care of yourself.

Remember, when you become a mother, you have a unique opportunity to learn from a whole lot of largely unavoidable mistakes—some that you'll laugh about and some that you'll cry about later on. You have a chance to develop true resilience, understanding yourself and your world more clearly in the process. You join a community of other women who have done the same and are stronger as a result. Lean into the opportunity. Learn to see it as a sometimes complicated but always beautiful journey, one that's exciting, and challenging, and life changing, all at the same time. Your children will thank you for it when they're navigating their own parenting paths years down the road.

Self-care Guides and Newborn Care Resources

Permission to reproduce the guides and resources for noncommercial purposes is granted with acknowledgment. For all other purposes, please contact the American Academy of Pediatrics to request permission.

Pediatrician Interview Questions

Use this space to jot down notes as you interview
potential pediatricians.

....

....

....

....

....

....

....

....

....

....

....

....

....

....

....

....

....

....

....

....

Caregiver Interview Questions

Use this space to write down notes as you interview potential caregivers for your baby. (Please see Nanny Sample Questionnaire and Child Care Center Sample Questionnaire on pages 73–75.)

Notes From My Hospital Tour

Use this space to write down notes as you tour the hospital
where you plan to deliver your baby.

Notes From My First Few Days of Motherhood

Use this space to write down your experience during your hospital stay and during your first few days at home with your new baby. Remember to look back on your reflections on your child's first birthday.

Questions for My Lactation Specialist

Use this space to write down questions about breastfeeding as they arise.

....

....

....

....

....

....

....

....

....

....

....

....

....

....

....

....

....

....

....

....

Questions for My Pediatrician

Use this space to write down questions about your baby's health in between pediatrician appointments.

Developing Priorities Guide

Following are activities we all spend time on, arranged randomly:

- Work
- Homemaking
- Kids
- Hobbies and sports
- Partner
- Appearance
- Friendships
- Exercise and stress reduction
- Travel and experiences

Rank these activities in order according to what you, in an ideal world, would spend the most time on or doing. Rank them as a private, honest list, not according to how you think other people would want you to rank them or how you think you should rank them.

IDEAL LIST

....

....

....

....

....

....

....

....

....

Now, rank the activities according to what you actually spend time on throughout the week or month.

REALITY LIST

....

....

....

....

....

....

....

....

Compare your first list (your ideal list) with the second list (your reality list). How do they match up? Use the top 3 items on your ideal list to help you determine a self-care ritual.

....

....

....

....

....

....

....

....

Partner Care Planning Guide

List several activities you and your partner each like to
do, individually.

YOU

....

....

....

....

PARTNER

....

....

....

....

List 4 experience activities you and your partner could
do locally together (think beyond dinner and a movie
[eg, concerts, hikes]).

....

....

....

....

List 4 bigger experience activities you and your partner could do together (eg, trips, events).

....

....

....

....

Potential child care options?

....

....

....

....

....

....

Potential barriers?

....

....

....

....

....

....

....

Self-care Goal Setting Guide

Self-care doesn't happen by luck; it happens by design. Follow these steps to make your self-care goals.

Reflect and evaluate

Think about what makes you happy in your life right now when it comes to self-care. Write out the top 5 things (your happy list) and then the top 5 things you wish were different (your wish list).

SAMPLE LISTS

Happy List

1. I enjoy special outings with my kids.

2. I see my friends once every 2 weeks at social, kid-related activities.

3. I have date nights with my husband occasionally.

4. I feel great when I take time to practice yoga or go for a walk outside.

5. My husband and I travel occasionally together.

Wish List

1. I want to be more physically fit.

2. I want to have more time when I'm quiet without distractions.

3. I want to travel more often.

4. I want to pursue my passions, things I used to spend time on before I had kids (writing, learning guitar, and learning about cooking).

5. I want to have more energy throughout the day.

YOUR LISTS

Happy List

1.

2.

3.

4.

5.

Wish List

1.

2.

3.

4.

5.

Set SMART goals

Then, set 3 SMART self-care goals based on your wish list: SMART goals are Specific, Measurable, Attainable, Realistic, and Time sensitive.

SPECIFIC

It's not worth it to have something like "I want to feel better about myself" as a goal. Feeling better is a good starting place, but it's just too ambiguous. There is no way to tell whether you've actually achieved your goal once you get there.

MEASURABLE

Measurable goals have an outcome you can assess after a certain amount of time to determine your level of progress. That way, you know when you've met your goal and are ready to set a new goal.

ATTAINABLE

If you set a goal that is too far out of reach, the chances of you reaching that goal are pretty slim. For example, an unattainable goal for me would be "I will be a marathon runner next month." Instead, "I will complete a 10K run in 3 months" is not so daunting.

REALISTIC

Realistic goals are goals that are not based in fantasy. Instead, they are possible to achieve, even if it takes several steps to accomplish them. For example, I could set a self-care goal of going to Italy 5 times a year, but I know that's not going to happen (I can't take that much time off work, I don't have the money for it, and I wouldn't have the child care resources for it). A more realistic goal? Going out of town with my husband (to a local venue or somewhere a short plane trip away) 3 times per year. We may have to save money to do it or I might have to work a little extra to make it happen, but it's something that I know is not completely far-fetched if I plan ahead and make it a priority.

TIME SENSITIVE

Even with self-care goals, time is an important element. If my desire is to be more physically fit and my goal is to work out more to achieve that desire, I need to set a timeline, so that I can get organized and motivate myself to actually make the change. For example, "My goal is to write a children's book by 1 year from now. I'll do step x by 1 month from now, step y by 2 months from now, and step z by 3 months from now to work toward that goal."

Breaking our goals into smaller steps makes it even more likely we'll achieve them.

STEP 1

....

....

....

....

....

....

....

....

....

STEP 2

....

....

....

....

....

....

....

....

....

Daily Baby Breastfeeding Log

Use this log to keep track of your baby's feedings, stools, and urinations.

Date	Time	Breast		Duration	Notes
		Right	Left		

Circle an *S* (soiled) when your baby passes stools and a *W* (wet) when your baby urinates.

S S S S S S S S S S S S S S S S S S S S S S S S

W W W W W W W W W W W W W W W W W W W

Daily Baby Breastfeeding Log (*continued*)

Use this log to keep track of your baby's feedings, stools, and urinations.

Date	Time	Breast		Duration	Notes
		Right	Left		

Circle an *S* (soiled) when your baby passes stools and a *W* (wet) when your baby urinates.

S S S S S S S S S S S S S S S S S S S S S S S

W W W W W W W W W W W W W W W W W W W W W W

Fussy Newborn Checklist

When your baby is fussy, first remember to consider these common reasons a baby can be uncomfortable or crying.

☐ Needs to feed

☐ Needs a diaper change

☐ Needs to burp

☐ Is overstimulated—needs to be calmed

☐ Is tired—needs to be soothed to sleep

If your newborn won't calm with these basic care techniques, call your pediatrician for help. If your baby has persistent fast or labored breathing or has a fever of 100.4°F (38°C) or higher, call your pediatrician's office immediately.

Emergency and Support Contact List

List the members in your immediate support circle (friends and family you can call for advice or help) as well as your emergency contacts. Keep this list on your refrigerator for easy access.

Hospital phone number:

....

Pediatrician phone number:

....

Lactation specialist phone number:

....

Support person number 1:

....

Support person number 2:

....

Support person number 3:

....

Support person number 4:

....

Breastfeeding Resources

- ## American Academy of Pediatrics (AAP)
  ## www.HealthyChildren.org

  The AAP is an organization of 67,000 primary care pediatricians, pediatric medical subspecialists, and pediatric surgical specialist dedicated to the health, safety, and well-being of infants, children, adolescents, and young adults. Its official website for parents, HealthyChildren.org, offers trustworthy, up-to-the-minute health care information and guidance for parents. Find a vast library of articles on breastfeeding from AAP experts designed to help families become more informed and find answers to common breastfeeding questions.

- ## Centers for Disease Control and Prevention "Breastfeeding" Pages
  ## www.cdc.gov/breastfeeding

  Includes basic information about breastfeeding, such as the safety of vaccinating pregnant women, traveling and breastfeeding, and other helpful information about breastfeeding and disease prevention.

- ## International Lactation Consultant Association (ILCA)
  ## www.ilca.org

  ILCA is the professional organization of lactation consultants and may be able to provide assistance with locating a lactation consultant in your area.

- ## La Leche League International (LLLI)
  ## www.llli.org

  Offers many resources for families including breastfeeding help, explanations of breastfeeding laws, breastfeeding publications, links to local LLLI leaders and groups, and more.

Developmental Milestones for Developmental Surveillance at Preventive Care Visits[a]

Age	Social Language and Self-help	Verbal Language (Expressive and Receptive)	Gross Motor	Fine Motor
Newborn–1 week	Makes brief eye contact with adult when held	Cries with discomfort Calms to adult voice	Reflexively moves arms and legs Turns head to side when on stomach	Holds fingers closed Grasps reflexively
1 month	Calms when picked up or spoken to Looks briefly at objects	Alerts to unexpected sound Makes brief short vowel sounds	Holds chin up in prone	Holds fingers more open at rest
2 months	Smiles responsively (ie, social smile)	Vocalizes with simple cooing	Lifts head and chest in prone	Opens and shuts hands
4 months	Laughs aloud	Turns to voice Vocalizes with extended cooing	Rolls over prone to supine Supports on elbows and wrists in prone	Keeps hands unfisted Plays with fingers in midline Grasps object
6 months	Pats or smiles at reflection Begins to turn when name called	Babbles	Rolls over supine to prone Sits briefly without support	Reaches for objects and transfers Rakes small object with 4 fingers Bangs small object on surface

continued

Developmental Milestones for Developmental Surveillance at Preventive Care Visits[a] (continued)

Age	Social Language and Self-help	Verbal Language (Expressive and Receptive)	Gross Motor	Fine Motor
9 months[b]	Uses basic gestures (holds arms out to be picked up, waves "bye-bye") Looks for dropped objects Picks up food with fingers and eats it Turns when name called	Says "Dada" or "Mama" nonspecifically	Sits well without support Pulls to stand Transitions well between sitting and lying Balances on hands and knees Crawls	Picks up small object with 3 fingers and thumb Releases objects intentionally Bangs objects together
12 months	Looks for hidden objects Imitates new gestures	Says "Dada" or "Mama" specifically Uses 1 word other than Mama, Dada, or personal names Follows a verbal command that includes a gesture	Takes first independent steps Stands without support	Drops object in a cup Picks up small object with 2-finger pincer grasp
15 months	Imitates scribbling Drinks from cup with little spilling Points to ask for something or to get help	Uses 3 words other than names Speaks in jargon Follows a verbal command without a gesture	Squats to pick up objects Climbs onto furniture Begins to run	Makes mark with crayon Drops object in and takes object out of a container

Age				
18 months[b,c]	Engages with others for play Helps dress and undress self Points to pictures in book Points to object of interest to draw attention to it Turns and looks at adult if something new happens Begins to scoop with spoon	Uses 6–10 words other than names Identifies at least 2 body parts	Walks up with 2 feet per step with hand held Sits in small chair Carries toy while walking	Scribbles spontaneously Throws small ball a few feet while standing
2 years[c]	Plays alongside other children (parallel) Takes off some clothing Scoops well with spoon	Uses 50 words Combines 2 words into short phrase or sentence Follows 2-step command Uses words that are 50% intelligible to strangers	Kicks ball Jumps off ground with 2 feet Runs with coordination	Stacks objects Turns book pages Uses hands to turn objects (eg, knobs, toys, and lids)
2½ years[b]	Urinates in a potty or toilet Engages in pretend or imitative play Spears food with fork	Uses pronouns correctly	Begins to walk up steps—alternating feet Runs well without falling	Grasps crayon with thumb and fingers instead of fist Catches large balls

continued

Developmental Milestones for Developmental Surveillance at Preventive Care Visits[a] (continued)

Age	Social Language and Self-help	Verbal Language (Expressive and Receptive)	Gross Motor	Fine Motor
3 years	Enters bathroom and urinates by self Plays in cooperation and shares Puts on coat, jacket, or shirt by self Engages in beginning imaginative play Eats independently	Uses 3-word sentences Uses words that are 75% intelligible to strangers Understands simple prepositions (eg, on, under)	Pedals tricycle Climbs on and off couch or chair Jumps forward	Draws a single circle Draws a person with head and 1 other body part Cuts with child scissors
4 years	Enters bathroom and has bowel movement by self Brushes teeth Dresses and undresses without much help Engages in well-developed imaginative play	Uses 4-word sentences Uses words that are 100% intelligible to strangers	Climbs stairs alternating feet without support Skips on 1 foot	Draws a person with at least 3 body parts Draws simple cross Unbuttons and buttons medium-sized buttons Grasps pencil with thumb and fingers instead of fist

[a] Developmental milestones are intended for discussion with parents for the purposes of surveillance of a child's developmental progress and for developmental promotion for the child. They are not intended or validated for use as a developmental screening test in the pediatric medical home or in early childhood day care or educational settings. Milestones are also commonly used for instructional purposes on early child development for pediatric and child development professional trainees.

These milestones generally represent the mean or average age of performance of these skills when available. When not available, the milestones offered are based on review and consensus from multiple measures as noted.

[b] It is recommended that a standardized developmental test be performed at these visits.

[c] It is recommended that a standardized autism screening test be performed at these visits.

Sources: Capute AJ, Shapiro BK, Palmer FB, Ross A, Wachtel RC. Normal gross motor development: the influences of race, sex and socio-economic status. *Dev Med Child Neurol.* 1985;27(5):635–643; Accardo PJ, Capute AJ. *The Capute Scales: Cognitive Adaptive Test/Clinical Linguistic and Auditory Milestone Scale (CAT/CLAMS).* Baltimore, MD: Paul H. Brookes Publishing Co; 2005; Beery KE, Buktenica NA, Beery NA. *The Beery-Buktenica Developmental Test of Visual-Motor Integration, Sixth Edition (BEERY VMI).* San Antonio, TX: Pearson Education Inc; 2010; Schum TR, Kolb TM, McAuliffe TL, Simms MD, Underhill RL, Lewis M. Sequential acquisition of toilet-training skills: a descriptive study of gender and age differences in normal children. *Pediatrics.* 2002;109(3):E48; Oller JW Jr, Oller SD, Oller SN. *Milestones: Normal Speech and Language Development Across the Lifespan.* 2nd ed. San Diego, CA: Plural Publishing Inc; 2012; Robins DL, Casagrande K, Barton M, Chen CM, Dumont-Mathieu T, Fein D. Validation of the Modified Checklist for Autism in Toddlers, Revised with Follow-Up (M-CHAT-R/F). *Pediatrics.* 2014;133(1):37–45; Aylward GP. *Bayley Infant Neurodevelopmental Screener.* San Antonio, TX: The Psychological Corporation; 1995; Squires J, Bricker D. *Ages & Stages Questionnaires, Third Edition (ASQ-3): A Parent-Completed Child Monitoring System.* Baltimore, MD: Paul H. Brookes Publishing Co; 2009; and Bly L. *Motor Skills Acquisition Checklist.* Psychological Corporation; 2000.

Suggested citation: Lipkin P, Macias M. Developmental milestones for developmental surveillance at preventive care visits. In: Hagan JF Jr, Shaw JS, Duncan PM, eds. *Bright Futures: Guidelines for Health Supervision of Infants, Children, and Adolescents.* 4th ed. Elk Grove Village, IL: American Academy of Pediatrics; 2017.

2019 Recommended Immunizations for Children from Birth Through 6 Years Old

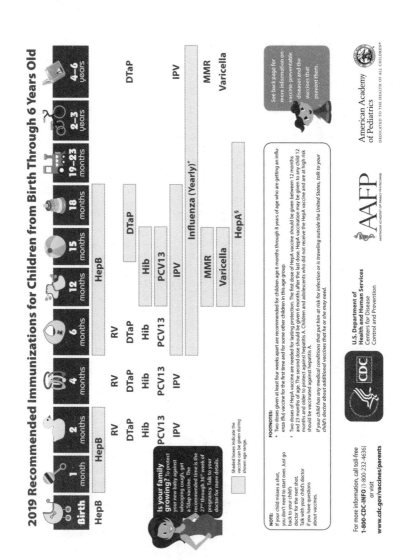

Birth	1 month	2 months	4 months	6 months	12 months	15 months	18 months	19–23 months	2–3 years	4–6 years
HepB	HepB				HepB					
		RV	RV	RV						
		DTaP	DTaP	DTaP		DTaP				DTaP
		Hib	Hib	Hib	Hib					
		PCV13	PCV13	PCV13	PCV13					
		IPV	IPV		IPV					IPV
					MMR	MMR				MMR
					Varicella	Varicella				Varicella
				Influenza (Yearly)*						
					HepA§					

Is your family growing? To protect your new baby against whooping cough, get a Tdap vaccine. The recommended time is the 27th through 36th week of pregnancy. Talk to your doctor for more details.

Shaded boxes indicate the vaccine can be given during shown age range.

NOTE:
If your child misses a shot, you don't need to start over. Just go back to your child's doctor for the next shot. Talk with your child's doctor if you have questions about vaccines.

FOOTNOTES:
* Two doses given at least four weeks apart are recommended for children age 6 months through 8 years of age who are getting an influenza (flu) vaccine for the first time and for some other children in this age group.

§ Two doses of HepA vaccine are needed for lasting protection. The first dose of HepA vaccine should be given between 12 months and 23 months of age. The second dose should be given 6 months after the last dose. HepA vaccination may be given to any child 12 months and older to protect against hepatitis A. Children and adolescents who did not receive the HepA vaccine and are at high risk should be vaccinated against hepatitis A.

If your child has any medical conditions that put him at risk for infection or is traveling outside the United States, talk to your child's doctor about additional vaccines that he or she may need.

See back page for more information on vaccine-preventable diseases and the vaccines that prevent them.

For more information, call toll-free
1-800-CDC-INFO (1-800-232-4636)
or visit
www.cdc.gov/vaccines/parents

U.S. Department of Health and Human Services
Centers for Disease Control and Prevention

CDC

AAFP
AMERICAN ACADEMY OF FAMILY PHYSICIANS

American Academy of Pediatrics
DEDICATED TO THE HEALTH OF ALL CHILDREN®

Vaccine-Preventable Diseases and the Vaccines that Prevent Them

Disease	Vaccine	Disease spread by	Disease symptoms	Disease complications
Chickenpox	Varicella vaccine protects against chickenpox.	Air, direct contact	Rash, tiredness, headache, fever	Infected blisters, bleeding disorders, encephalitis (brain swelling), pneumonia (infection in the lungs)
Diphtheria	DTaP* vaccine protects against diphtheria.	Air, direct contact	Sore throat, mild fever, weakness, swollen glands in neck	Swelling of the heart muscle, heart failure, coma, paralysis, death
Hib	Hib vaccine protects against *Haemophilus influenzae* type b.	Air, direct contact	May be no symptoms unless bacteria enter the blood	Meningitis (infection of the covering around the brain and spinal cord), intellectual disability, epiglottitis (life-threatening infection that can block the windpipe and lead to serious breathing problems), pneumonia (infection in the lungs), death
Hepatitis A	HepA vaccine protects against hepatitis A.	Direct contact, contaminated food or water	May be no symptoms, fever, stomach pain, loss of appetite, fatigue, vomiting, jaundice (yellowing of skin and eyes), dark urine	Liver failure, arthralgia (joint pain), kidney, pancreatic and blood disorders
Hepatitis B	HepB vaccine protects against hepatitis B.	Contact with blood or body fluids	May be no symptoms, fever, headache, weakness, vomiting, jaundice (yellowing of skin and eyes), joint pain	Chronic liver infection, liver failure, liver cancer
Influenza (Flu)	Flu vaccine protects against influenza.	Air, direct contact	Fever, muscle pain, sore throat, cough, extreme fatigue	Pneumonia (infection in the lungs)
Measles	MMR** vaccine protects against measles.	Air, direct contact	Rash, fever, cough, runny nose, pink eye	Encephalitis (brain swelling), pneumonia (infection in the lungs), death
Mumps	MMR**vaccine protects against mumps.	Air, direct contact	Swollen salivary glands (under the jaw), fever, headache, tiredness, muscle pain	Meningitis (infection of the covering around the brain and spinal cord), encephalitis (brain swelling), inflammation of testicles or ovaries, deafness
Pertussis	DTaP* vaccine protects against pertussis (whooping cough).	Air, direct contact	Severe cough, runny nose, apnea (a pause in breathing in infants)	Pneumonia (infection in the lungs), death
Polio	IPV vaccine protects against polio.	Air, direct contact; through the mouth	May be no symptoms, sore throat, fever, nausea, headache	Paralysis, death
Pneumococcal	PCV13 vaccine protects against pneumococcus.	Air, direct contact	May be no symptoms, pneumonia (infection in the lungs)	Bacteremia (blood infection), meningitis (infection of the covering around the brain and spinal cord), death
Rotavirus	RV vaccine protects against rotavirus.	Through the mouth	Diarrhea, fever, vomiting	Severe diarrhea, dehydration
Rubella	MMR** vaccine protects against rubella.	Air, direct contact	Sometimes rash, fever, swollen lymph nodes	Very serious in pregnant women—can lead to miscarriage, stillbirth, premature delivery, birth defects
Tetanus	DTaP* vaccine protects against tetanus.	Exposure through cuts in skin	Stiffness in neck and abdominal muscles, difficulty swallowing, muscle spasms, fever	Broken bones, breathing difficulty, death

* DTaP combines protection against diphtheria, tetanus, and pertussis.
** MMR combines protection against measles, mumps, and rubella.

Last updated January 2019 • CS300526-A

Index